baked liss...

THE
LITTLE BEAN
BOOK

THE LITTLE BEAN BOOK

by

Margie F. Tyler

QUAIL RIDGE PRESS

Brandon, Mississippi

1989

DEDICATION

This book is dedicated to all the bean lovers across the country and to those friends who contributed to this collection. The encouragement and support of my family are gratefully acknowledged.

The Hinds County (Mississippi) Home Extension Department, the Mississippi Soybean Association, and the Idaho-Washington Dry Pea and Lentil Commission were especially helpful in supplying information and tested recipes.

Copyright 1989 by
Quail Ridge Press, Inc.

All Rights Reserved

Manufactured in the United States of America

First printing, September 1989

Library of Congress Catalog Card Number: 89-42868

Library of Congress Cataloging-in-Publication Data

Tyler, Margie F.
The little bean book / Margie F. Tyler.
p.   cm.
Includes index.
ISBN 0-937552-32-1 : $9.95
1. Cookery (Beans) 2. Cookery, American.   I. Title.
TX803.B4T95   1989
641 . 6'565--dc20   89-42868

TABLE OF CONTENTS

Foreword   6

In Flavor of the Bean   7

The Bean Connection   9

Peas in the Pot. 13

Appetizers 15

Soups and Sauces. 21

Salads. 37

Baked Beans 47

Main and Side Dishes 53

Sweets. 85

Miscellaneous. 91

Tables. 96

Index 99

About the Author 104

FOREWORD

The first introduction to cooking took place in the kitchen of my grandfather's hotel, the Southern Hotel in Tupelo, Mississippi. I had a special stool by the table that Chef Jeff presided over. There was always lots of noise in the kitchen, lots of movement, and even some shouting, but what came out of that warm, steamy room tantalizes in memory to this day. I never order pancakes that I don't wish for Jeff's, because they were so light they surely could have floated to heaven.

My own style of cooking has been greatly influenced by having lived as a child in seven southeastern states. Most of the time our family was blessed with a cook in the kitchen, so I had firsthand knowledge of Cajun food in Louisiana, the Tex-Mex of Oklahoma and Texas, and the wonderful creamy flavors of the Deep South. In later years I have experienced food from my travels across the United States as well as my trips to Europe. Eating is such an adventure—a chance to explore new tastes native to a region or a country. Many recipes and methods have been given to me by gracious chefs. Some even allowed me into their realm of the kitchen.

A few years ago I began to enter cooking competitions and have been fortunate to have cooked in five national events. Creating original recipes is an adventure in itself.

This involvement and interest in food finally evolved to this book. But why the bean book? When a high cholesterol count led me to a change in diet, I became interested in this wonder food, the bean. After three months of menus filled with oats and beans, my count dropped to a safe level and I became a real believer in this nutritional sleeping giant! It is truly the food of the '90s because of its remarkable health benefits.

I hope this collection of bean recipes will encourage you to include beans on your shopping list as often as you do potatoes. Feel free to experiment and create your own dishes. This could be the beginning of something good!

Margie Tyler

IN FLAVOR OF THE BEAN

Bean cooking encompasses much more than the black-eyed peas on New Year's Day, Deep South red beans and rice, Boston baked beans, or the bean soup of the House and Senate. A quick look at the index will reveal the wealth of recipes that exist from regional cooking, plus new versions of old favorite ways of cooking beans, peas, lentils, and a legume we love, the peanut.

The good-tasting foods on the following pages exemplify the variety and versatility of beans. To help you discover the wonders of these legumes, recipes have been chosen that are easily prepared with ingredients readily available. Today's supermarkets offer us a broad variety of beans, peas, and lentils, dried as well as fresh, and available year round. Occasionally a recipe will call for an ingredient best found at a health food store, but the extra effort will reward you in discovering many new approaches to food preparation.

Nutritionists, dietitians, and doctors have begun to concentrate on the importance of food habits in the fight against heart disease, cancer, and diabetes. The recognition that low-fat and cholesterol-free diets can save lives has raised the lowly bean to superstar status because it meets all requirements: legumes contain no cholesterol; fat content is polyunsaturated (the good fat); they are rich in B vitamins including thiamine and niacin, contain iron and potassium, and are low in sodium. When legumes are served with C-rich fruits or foods, almost all of the amino acid requirements are met. There is every reason to say 'a bean a day will keep the doctor away.'

Besides being cholesterol-free, dried beans contain essential fiber needed to create bulk in the intestinal tract. Dietary fiber has

7

been linked with lower risk of colon cancer, weight loss, and reduced cholesterol. One-half cup of dried beans can furnish 7.5 grams of fiber. (The recommended level is 25-30 grams a day.)

A doctor first introduced peanut butter when a patient needed a digestible source of protein. The good doctor creamed peanuts and discovered you did not have to be ill to enjoy the dish. The noted scientist, George Washington Carver, is credited with finding over 200 uses of the peanut, and early preached the health benefits of this unlikely-named legume.

Carbon-dated specimens reveal that beans were on the European continent as early as 5500 B.C., and dried peas were eaten as far back as 9500 B.C. in Burma, Thailand, and China. Lentils are referred to in the book of Genesis; early Greeks used lentils as a curative food as well as an aphrodisiac. But most of the varieties of beans used in the United States came through explorers of South America, particularly Peru, and from early settlers from European countries. One tale tells us that the Indians taught the New England pioneers the art of cooking beans with bear meat. Maple syrup was added by our early cooks to make the dish more palatable.

Botanically speaking, the bean is a pulse belonging to the plant family, leguminosae. The fruit or pod of these plants produces seeds that we know as beans, peas, lentils and peanuts. The peanut is a strange legume, producing its pods underground.

Regardless of what you call this remarkable food—pulse, legume, or bean—this low-cost source of protein and good taste is as close as your grocery cart.

A publication of our American Heart Association says it best: 'Making the decision to adopt a low-fat, healthful eating plan is making a good investment...with both immediate and long-term benefits.'

'Full of beans?' You bet. Full of vigor and vitality! 'Looks like a bean pole?' Great! Thin, slim and healthy! So use your 'bean'—eat beans; they are not just *good*—they are *good for you.*

Enjoy!

8

THE BEAN CONNECTION

Although there are over 30 different varieties of legumes, we are listing only those commonly used in this collection. We have included a number of recipes of by-products of beans, mainly from the soybean, and several others that you might find on the shelf.

Most recipes adapt to substitution very well, especially with dried peas and beans. Lentils cook very quickly and usually it is best to follow closely the recipe calling for lentils.

There are also several varieties of black and red beans found most often in ethnic or health food stores, but these are also interchangeable with our more common varieties found in local markets.

Black beans, native to South America, Cuba, and Central America, are oval shaped, rather small and shiny. Used mostly in black bean soup and beans and rice, it is often flavored with coriander or oregano to aid in digestion.

Black-eyed peas are creamy-white, small kidney-shaped beans with black eye, hence the name. They are sweet tasting, and cook quickly, so they do not require overnight soaking. Greeks use this bean about as much as southern Americans. Another name for this bean is cowpea.

Broad beans are sometimes known as horse beans. They are large, can be green-brown, and require long soaking because of coarse husks. They can be bought canned or fresh.

9

Butter beans, also called Fordhook, are buttery flavored, and served as often fresh as dried. They may be green or white. In the South the term is used interchangeably with lima beans. White beans are smaller and more often served from fresh or frozen beans.

Chickpeas (garbanzos) are round tan legumes which often find themselves on American salad bars. In Italy, where they are called ceci, they are used in stews, soups, and spreads. The Middle Eastern dish, Hummus, is a popular dip. Do not eat garbanzos raw—a toxin may cause digestive problems.

Cranberry beans are sometimes called Roman Beans, though Italians call them Borlottis. New England recipes call for this reddish streaked little bean. Their color makes them attractive in salads and mixed dishes.

Great northern beans (or Cannellini) are native to South America and the only source if you are to be authentic, but this white kidney bean is related to the haricot and is easily interchangeable.

Navy beans (or haricots) are small, white, oval-shaped beans used in traditional baked bean recipes, soups, and stews. They are quick soaking and 1 1/2 hours of boiling has them ready to eat. They cream well for dips, too.

The name **lentils** comes from the convex lentil shape of this legume. Once you get the taste of lentils, they can't help but become a family favorite. They are tiny, come in three colors, and cook quickly without soaking.

Flageolets are small little kidney-shaped beans from France, and are often listed in French recipes. They are very expensive. You may read about them or be fortunate enough to dine on them.

Kidney beans are one of our most common beans and named for their shape. They are a lovely wine-red bean, used in chili, red beans and rice, and salads; and they are good canned and seasoned or cooked from 'scratch.'

Mung beans are used mostly for sprouting. This tiny moss-green bean can be cooked in less than two hours and is the base for many far Eastern and Indian dishes.

Peanuts (called a ground nut in Africa), are a truly important member of the legume family, growing only in the southern region. They are second to the soybean in nutritional value. You honestly can survive on peanut butter sandwiches and milk.

Pinto beans are a staple food in Mexico, found in many Tex-Mex dishes. They have a savory flavor, creamy texture, and are great for refried bean recipes.

Soya beans, a staple in Chinese cooking, are most commonly called soybeans. The most common use in North America is in soy sauce and products made for animal consumption. When you see the term 'other oils' on a bottle, it more than likely means soy oil. Ten percent of our babies use this milk to survive their allergy to cow's milk. This remarkable legume is 100 percent protein, and higher in fat content, but has so many pure qualities you wonder why we have not placed it in our food basket more often. It is possible to have a complete meal from soup, to bread, to main dish with this bean. It is an important crop in the South and subject to much study and experimentation.

Split peas: In Britain they call these peas *porridge*—but don't leave in the pot nine days—you would have a tipsy kettle of peas. Don't confuse yourself that these are fresh green peas split—these tiny little legumes just grow that way, flat on one side, and can be green or yellow. We use the green for wonderful split-pea soup. There is the whole pea from fresh green peas that is dried and used for soups and stews, but the two are not the same.

A WORD ABOUT PODS

In order to broaden the scope of this collection, a number of recipes for fresh or frozen pods are included below.

Chinese pea pods—snow peas, crisp green pods, with little humps of seeds showing—are used in Chinese dishes, stir-fried vegetable dishes, soups, and salads. They require little or no cooking, and a few go a long way.

Kentucky Wonder and green snap beans are those long and flat pods that are cooked as is. Many times at the end of the growing season, the cook will shell a few from mature pods and add to the pot. And when you let them hang on the vine, they can become Kentucky Shell-outs.

Fresh English or green peas are staple with most American cooks. An early spring treat but almost as good cooked from frozen. English peas are sweet, have a beautiful green color.

Tofu is soybean curd made from curdled soy milk, very much like cheese. Usually found in the fresh produce section packaged in water. Tofu must be refrigerated as it spoils easily. It is good used crumbled in salads or other foods because of its bland taste. It is an excellent source of needed proteins with a low calorie count.

Although mung beans are usually used for **bean sprouts,** other beans may be used (see recipe on p. 94). Bean sprouts are readily available at fresh produce counters. They are used in salads or Chinese dishes.

Soy sauce is a must for Asian dishes. Equal parts of soy beans and cracked roasted wheat with salt and water are allowed to ferment from 6 months to 5 years. Synthetic sauce is prepared from soy protein, corn syrup, and caramel coloring.

PEAS IN THE POT

Pease porridge hot,
Pease porridge cold,
Pease porridge in the pot
Nine days old.

Some like them hot,
Some like them cold,
Some like them in the pot
Nine days old.

ANONYMOUS

Not nine days old! Beans and peas can ferment within hours, so it is best to keep refrigerated even in the soaking period. The old nursery rhyme doesn't apply except in verse.

Basic preparation

Wash dried beans carefully, removing sediment and discolored pieces. Fresh peas and beans often have the same need. All beans should be rinsed through several washes. Remove any that float to the top.

Overnight soaking

Dried limas and navy beans usually require overnight soaking (or at least 4-6 hours), otherwise cooking time will be as much as 6 hours. It is possible that long soaking helps to prevent digestive problems that occur with some individuals, but most beans are ready for cooking after a 1 1/2 to 2-hour soaking period. Fresh beans and peas require no soaking.

Quick soaking

Place washed beans in a pan. Cover with water. Bring to a boil over high heat and boil for 2 minutes. Remove from heat and let sit covered for 2 hours.

Salt may be used in either soaking method. This cuts down on the amount of salt used in the cooking period and minimizes the risk of the beans fermenting.

13

Cooking Tips:

Lentils and split peas require no soaking period. To do so would leave you a pot of mush when cooked. It is also best not to stir a pot of cooking lentils for the same reason. Careful monitoring of the heat is a must.

For quick cooking, use the pressure cooker. Slow cooking of beans blends the flavors of spices, herbs, and other ingredients. But when a recipe calls for precooked beans, pressure cooking is a time-saver, unless, of course, you have canned beans on hand. Beans take very well to crockpot cooking, but you must be careful not to overcook with this method.

There is little time saved in microwave cooking except for canned or precooked beans and peas. Green beans can be cooked tender-crisp very well, but on the whole, cooking beans the conventional way is just as well.

Estimated Cooking Times:

Black-eyed peas	1 1/4 - 1 1/2 hours
Black beans	2 1/2 - 3 hours
Lima beans	3/4 - 1 hour
Navy beans	1 1/4 - 1 1/2 hours
Great northern beans	1 1/4 - 1 1/2 hours
Kidney beans	2 - 3 hours
Pinto beans	2 - 2 1/2 hours
Garbanzo beans (Chickpeas)	2 - 3 hours
Soybeans	4 - 6 hours

See page 96 for tables of equivalents, calories, weights, and measurements.

APPETIZERS

LUCKY BLACK-EYED PEA DIP
Start the New Year in southern party style!

1 stick margarine
1 (6-ounce) roll pasteurized
    processed garlic cheese
1 (6-ounce) roll pasteurized
    processed jalapeño cheese

2 (15.8-ounce) cans black-eyed
    peas
2 garlic cloves, minced
1 medium onion, diced
2 teaspoons diced jalapeño

Melt margarine and both cheese rolls in a casserole dish in the microwave on medium to low power (or melt over very low heat or in top of a double boiler). Drain peas and save liquid. Gently mash peas with a fork. Stir the garlic, onion, jalapeño and peas into the melted cheese. Thin with reserved liquid from peas if too thick. Serve warm with corn or tortilla chips. Makes about 4 cups.

SPICY BEAN DIP

1 (16-ounce) can kidney beans,
    drained
1 teaspoon cumin
1 teaspoon coriander
1 tablespoon vinegar

1 tablespoon lime juice
2 tablespoons finely minced
    onion
2 teaspoons parsley

Blend all ingredients except onion and parsley in a blender until smooth. Transfer to serving bowl. Garnish with onions and parsley. Serve with Mexican-type chips. Makes 1 1/2 cups.

15

HUMMUS

This traditional Mid-eastern dish is used as a dip for fresh vegetables, served on pita bread for a main dish, or as a sauce for vegetable and bean dishes.

2 garlic cloves, minced
1/2 cup minced, onions
1 tablespoon olive oil
2 cups cooked chickpeas
(garbanzos)

1/2 cup lemon juice
1 tablespoon soy sauce
1/2 cup sesame seeds

Sauté garlic and onions in hot oil until onions are wilted. Purée chickpeas in food processor or blender. Blend in onion and garlic, lemon juice, soy sauce and sesame seeds. Makes about 3 cups.

GREEK BEAN DIP

1 (16-ounce) can white navy beans,
drained (reserve 3 tablespoons
liquid)
1 tablespoon chopped onion
1 clove garlic, minced

1/2 teaspoon chili powder
1/2 teaspoon ground cumin
1/2 cup grated Cheddar cheese
2 tablespoons olive oil
4 pita breads, cut in quarters

Combine all ingredients except cheese and pita breads in blender with reserved bean juice. Blend until smooth. Transfer to 1-quart saucepan; add cheese and cook on slow heat, stirring constantly, until cheese melts. Transfer to chafing dish. Serve with pita breads. Makes about 2 1/2 - 3 cups.

BLACK BEAN DIP

1 tablespoon butter or margarine
1/2 cup chopped onion
1 large garlic clove, minced

2 cups black beans, cooked or
canned
1 cup sour cream

Heat butter; sauté onion and garlic until tender. Add onion mixture to beans and purée in blender. Place bean mixture in large bowl. Cover and chill several hours. Before serving, stir in sour cream. Serve with assorted cut vegetables. Makes 2 cups.

MISSISSIPPI CAVIAR

1 (15.8-ounce) can black-eyed peas	1 medium onion, finely chopped
1/2 cup minced hot green chilies	1/4 cup olive oil
1 garlic clove, finely minced	1/4 cup white vinegar

Drain peas in a colander, rinse, and pat dry. Mix all ingredients in bowl. Refrigerate overnight. Let stand at room temperature and stir well before serving with crackers or corn chips. Makes about 3 cups.
Variation: Substitute 1 can drained pinto beans for black-eyed peas.

REFRIED-BEAN PARTY DIP

1 can refried beans	2 jalapeño peppers, sliced
2 sticks butter	1 medium onion, grated
1 cup grated sharp cheese	1 clove garlic, minced

Heat all ingredients in double boiler, adding desired amount of liquid from peppers; cook, stirring until cheese melts. Serve in chafing dish with corn chips. Makes 2 1/2 - 3 cups.

MEXICALI BEAN DIP

1/3 cup olive oil	1/8 teaspoon thyme
1 small onion, chopped	1/2 teaspoon dry mustard
1 chili pepper, minced	2 tablespoons brown sugar
1 pod garlic, minced	2 cups canned red beans, drained
2 cups canned tomatoes, drained	2 teaspoons minced parsley for
1 teaspoon chili powder	garnish

Heat oil, then sauté onions, pepper, and garlic until tender. Add tomatoes, seasonings and sugar. Simmer 5 minutes. Mash beans until smooth. Stir in tomato mixture. Serve in chafing dish. Sprinkle parsley as garnish. Serve with tortilla chips and crackers. Makes about 6 cups.

STUFFED SNOW PEAS
An elegant party pick-up food that is good for you.

1/2 pound snow peas

Wash snow peas. Split on top side to form small boat. Blanch in salted boiling water for several seconds. Then cool in a bowl of water and ice, dipping once. Remove, drain and set aside to cool. Stuff with filling: shrimp, crabmeat, cream cheese-chive or any variety of seasoned cream cheese filling.

SHRIMP FILLING:

1 small can shrimp, well-drained	**3 dashes Tabasco sauce**
1/2 cup soft cream cheese	**3 tablespoons minced onion**
4 tablespoons mayonnaise	

Mix ingredients gently to keep shrimp whole.

CREAM CHEESE AND CHIVES:

1 (8-ounce) carton cream cheese	**2 tablespoons chives**
1/2 cup mayonnaise	**1 teaspoon salt**
1 teaspoon capers	

Serves 6-8 (20 snow pea appetizers).

CHICKPEA SPREAD FOR CANAPÉS

1 3/4 cups cooked chickpeas or	**1 tablespoon mayonnaise**
garbanzo beans (save liquid)	**1/4 teaspoon garlic powder**
2 tablespoons lemon juice	

Drain chickpeas, saving liquid. Mash and blend chickpeas. Add 1 tablespoon liquid and lemon juice, mayonnaise and garlic powder. Mix until smooth. If too thick, add chickpea liquid. Makes about 2 cups.

Variation: Beans in the recipe can be canned or cooked from dry beans. To cook dry beans, cover with 3 times as much water as beans. Soak overnight. Drain. Add 3 quarts water. Cook 1 1/2 - 2 hours.

18

BLACK-EYED PEA NACHOS

2 (about 1-pound) cans black-eyed
peas (can use jalapeño seasoned
peas) or cooked peas
48 round tostado chips

1/2 pound shredded Cheddar
cheese
Jalapeño slices (optional)
Picante sauce

Heat black-eyed peas and mash coarsely (can blend partially in blender and coarsely chop remainder to add texture). Spread on tostados. Sprinkle with cheese and jalapeños. Top with picante sauce. If desired, heat in microwave or toaster oven until cheese is slightly melted.

Variation: Place mashed black-eyed peas in bowl; top with cheese, jalapeños and picante sauce and serve surrounded by tostado chips or crisp tortilla pieces for dipping.

PEANUT BALLS

1 tablespoon vegetable oil
2 tablespoons flour
2 tablespoons milk
1/2 teaspoon salt
1/4 teaspoon pepper
1/8 teaspoon paprika

2 cups cooked rice
1 cup ground peanuts
1 egg, beaten
Beaten egg and bread crumbs
Oil for frying

Make a roux from heated oil, flour, milk and seasonings. Do not let the roux brown. Set aside. Mix rice, roux, peanuts and beaten egg. Shape into small balls. Sauté in hot oil until brown on all sides or dip in beaten egg and bread crumbs and deep-fat fry until brown. Makes 10-12 balls depending on size.

NIGERIAN BEAN BALLS

1 cup cooked black-eyed peas
1 teaspoon salt
Pepper to taste

1 large onion, finely chopped
Cooking fat

Mash peas until smooth, add salt, pepper, onion. Shape into 8-10 small balls. Fry in hot oil until brown on both sides.

19

BEAN SPREAD FOR COCKTAIL CRACKERS

2 cups cooked white beans (navy or chickpeas) well-drained	1 teaspoon onion flakes
1 tablespoon red wine vinegar	1 teaspoon chopped chives
2 tablespoons olive oil	1 teaspoon parsley flakes
	1/4 teaspoon each salt, pepper

Mash beans thoroughly; gradually add vinegar and oil. Fold in remaining ingredients. Mixture should be of spreading consistency. Add additional drops of oil if necessary. Spread on rounds of cocktail rye bread or crackers. Sprinkle with paprika. Makes about 2 cups.

Variation: Make corn bread in mini-muffin pans. Split, toast, then spread with bean mixture. Serve warm.

GREEN BEAN CANAPÉS

Have plenty of these tasty little sandwiches in reserve—they are a real party favorite.

1 can vertical-packed whole string beans	1 loaf fresh, thin-sliced bread
1 (8-ounce) bottle Italian dressing	1 (3-ounce) package cream cheese, softened
1 garlic clove, minced	1/2 cup mayonnaise
1 teaspoon oregano	1 teaspoon chives

Drain beans. Mix Italian dressing, garlic and oregano. Pour over beans. Cover and refrigerate overnight.

Trim bread of crusts. Mix cream cheese, mayonnaise and chives. Spread one slice of bread with cream cheese mixture. Place 1 bean on bread. Roll up jelly roll fashion and secure with a toothpick. Place in large flat container roll side down. Continue spreading bread slices until all beans are used. Sprinkle with paprika and chill several hours before serving. (Makes as many sandwiches as number of beans per can.)

SOUPS
AND
SAUCES

ITALIAN BEAN SOUP WITH PASTA

1/2 cup dry navy beans
1 1/2 cups dry yellow or green
  split peas
2 (12-ounce) cans tomato juice
1/2 cup chopped onion
1/2 cup sliced celery
1 cup cubed zucchini
2 cups coarsely chopped cabbage
1 cup diced turnip

1 cup diced carrots
1 garlic clove, minced
1 teaspoon salt
1/2 teaspoon pepper
3/4 teaspoon Italian seasoning
2 ounces spaghetti, uncooked,
  broken in quarters
8 tablespoons Parmesan cheese

Soak beans in 3 1/2 cups water overnight or use the quick-soak method: Bring beans to a boil in 3 1/2 cups water and boil gently for 1 minute. Cover pan and let stand for 2 hours.

Resume recipe: Add 8 1/4 cups more water. Add peas and bring to a boil. Reduce heat. Cover and simmer 1 hour or until peas and beans are tender.

Add remaining ingredients except spaghetti and cheese. Cook until vegetables are tender. Add spaghetti and cook an additional 8-10 minutes until spaghetti is tender. Sprinkle with cheese before serving. Serves 8.

BLACK-EYED PEA SOUP

1 pound dried black-eyed peas
(2 1/2 cups)
3 quarts water
5 slices bacon, cut in small pieces
1 cup medium chopped yellow
onion
1 tablespoon chopped jalapeños

2 cups chopped fresh tomatoes
2 teaspoons minced garlic
1/2 teaspoon salt
1/4 teaspoon pepper
2 beef bouillon cubes
1 1/2 cups grated Cheddar cheese

Rinse peas. Place in large pot; cover with water and bring to boil. Turn off heat and let sit 1-3 hours.
Drain and add 3 quarts fresh water. In heavy skillet, brown bacon; add onion, jalapeños, tomatoes, garlic, and salt and pepper. Dissolve bouillon cubes in mixture. Add these ingredients to pot of peas. Bring to boil, then turn to simmer for 2 hours, or until peas are tender.
Stir in cheese and simmer gently until cheese is melted. Yields about 6-8 servings.

VEGETABLE SOYBEAN SOUP

2 tablespoons oil
2 onions, chopped
1 clove garlic, chopped
2 carrots, peeled and sliced
1 green pepper, diced
2 ribs celery, diced
2 cups canned tomatoes with
juice
1 cup whole kernel corn

1/4 head (small) cabbage,
chopped
1/2 teaspoon thyme
2 teaspoons dried parsley
flakes
2 quarts beef broth
1 1/2 cups cooked soybeans
(1 pound drained, divided)
Salt and pepper to taste

Heat oil in small skillet; sauté onions and garlic until tender. Drain. Place vegetables in 4-quart saucepan with beef broth and onion mixture. Mash 1/2 cup of soybeans into mixture. Season. Bring to boil, then turn to simmer; cover pot and cook until vegetables are tender. Add remaining up of soybeans. Simmer an additional 10 minutes. Serves 8-10.

THREE-BEAN SOUP WITH CRAB BOIL

1/2 cup each: dried kidney beans,
    black-eyed peas, navy beans
3 quarts water
1/2 pound lean ham hock
1/2 teaspoon salt

1/4 teaspoon pepper
1 bay leaf
1/2 cup rice
Liquid crab boil to taste

Wash beans carefully. Place in 4-quart Dutch oven with water; add ham hock, salt, pepper, bay leaf, and rice. Bring to boil, turn to simmer, and cook 2 hours or until beans are tender. Add crab boil to taste; cook additional 20 minutes. Remove bay leaf before serving. Garnish bowl with minced green onion. Yields 6-8 servings.

FRESH GREEN PEA SOUP

3 pounds fresh green peas, shelled
6 cups cold water
6 slices bacon
1 small onion, chopped
1/4 teaspoon sugar

2 tablespoons butter
Salt to taste
1/2 cup heavy cream
6 fresh snow peas, cut in slivers

In large saucepan, cover peas with cold water. Add bacon, onion, and sugar. Bring to boil; simmer until peas are tender, about 10-20 minutes. Remove bacon. Purée peas in blender. Add butter, salt and cream and heat, but do not boil. Thin with water if necessary.

Snip ends of snow peas. Blanch in salted boiling water for 2 minutes. Drain. Garnish soup with snow peas. Serves 4-6.

SPLIT PEA SOUP

1 cup dried split peas
2 quarts water
1 carrot, shredded
1 tablespoon chopped fresh
    parsley (or 1 1/2 teaspoons
    dried flakes)

1/2 teaspoon garlic powder
1/4 teaspoon rosemary
2 ribs celery, finely chopped
Salt and pepper to taste

Place all ingredients in a 4-quart saucepan. Cover and simmer 2-3 hours, adding water if soup becomes too thick. For creamier soup, place in blender; reheat before serving. Serves 6-8.

23

SPLIT PEA SOUP MILANO

1 cup split peas, rinsed and
  drained
5 cups water
5 bouillon cubes or teaspoon beef
  bouillon granules
Dash pepper
2 tablespoons olive oil
1/4 pound Italian sausage

1 cup chopped celery
1/2 cup chopped onion
1 clove garlic, minced
1/2 cup sweet red pepper,
  minced
1/4 cup dry red wine or hot water
Grated Parmesan cheese for
  garnish

In large saucepan or pot, combine peas, water, bouillon and pepper.
Heat to boiling, reduce heat to simmer. Cover and simmer until
peas are tender, stirring occasionally, about 30 minutes.

Meanwhile, in skillet over medium heat, cook sausage until no
longer pink, breaking into small crumbles with back of spoon. Add
celery, onion, garlic, and pepper and sauté until onion is tender and
translucent, about 5 minutes. Add sausage-vegetable mixture to
peas along with wine. Simmer 10-15 minutes to blend flavors.
Sprinkle with Parmesan cheese. Serves 5 or 6.

HADDOW SOUP

*A Greek fisherman's stew was the inspiration for this soup; but it is
worthy of being the first course for a sophisticated dinner party.*

1 can cream of tomato soup
1 can split pea soup
1 can chicken consommé
1/2 cup milk or cream
1 1/2 cups fresh or canned
  crabmeat, carefully picked over

1/2 teaspoon Worcestershire
  sauce
4 ounces sherry

Heat 3 soups in 4-quart container. Gradually stir in milk or cream,
crabmeat, and Worcestershire sauce. Add sherry just before placing
in serving bowls. Serves 6.

---

*Botanists rank dry peas and lentils second only to grasses in terms of their
importance to mankind.*

24

NEW ORLEANS RED BEAN SOUP

1 small onion, chopped
1/4 stick butter
1 gallon water
1/2 pound dried red beans
1/2 teaspoon ground cloves
2 garlic cloves
2 ribs celery, cut
2 bay leaves

2 sprigs thyme (or
  1 teaspoon dried)
1 teaspoon Worcestershire sauce
1/2 pound finely ground ham
Salt and pepper to taste
8 tablespoons sherry
2 hard-boiled eggs, sliced
8 thin lemon slices

In large pot, brown onions in butter. Add water, beans, cloves, garlic, celery, bay leaves, thyme, and Worcestershire sauce. Simmer 3-4 hours. Remove 1 cup beans, mash, return to pot. Add ham, salt, and pepper. Place 1 tablespoon sherry in bottom of each bowl before adding soup. Garnish with egg and lemon slices. Serves 8-12.

DELTA QUEEN BLACK BEAN SOUP

4 cups black beans
5 quarts (20-cups) chicken stock
3 ribs celery, finely chopped
3 large onions, chopped
8 tablespoons (1 stick) butter
2 1/2 tablespoons flour
1/2 cup parsley, chopped
Smoked ham bone with rind

3 leeks, thinly sliced
4 bay leaves
1 tablespoon salt
1/2 teaspoon ground pepper
1 cup Madeira wine
2 hard-boiled eggs, chopped
1 lemon, thinly sliced

Wash beans, cover with cold water and soak overnight. Drain. Add chicken stock and cook over low heat 1 hour. In large pot, sauté celery and onions in butter until tender. Blend in flour and parsley and cook for 1 minute. Gradually stir in beans and liquid. Add ham bone and rind, leeks, bay leaves, salt and pepper. Simmer over low heat 4 hours.

Remove ham bone and rind and bay leaves. Purée beans in food processor or blender, or force beans through sieve. Combine puréed beans and broth with Madeira. Bring soup to a boil, remove from heat and add hard-boiled eggs. Float a thin slice of lemon on each serving. Makes 12-16 servings.

Always remove bay leaves from bean dishes before serving.

BLACK BEAN PAPRIKA SOUP

1 pound black beans, soaked
  overnight
1 cup chopped onions
1/2 teaspoon basil
1/2 teaspoon oregano
1/4 teaspoon chili powder

1/4 teaspoon chili powder
1 teaspoon paprika
1 tablespoon sherry
Salt and pepper to taste
Feta cheese

Place soaked black beans in pot with 2 quarts water. Add remaining ingredients except cheese. Bring to a boil, then turn to medium heat and cook until beans are tender, 1 1/2 to 2 hours. Remove 1 scant cup of beans, mash, and return to pot. Season to taste. Serve with crumbled feta cheese on top. Serves 6-8.

CREOLE BLACK BEAN SOUP

1 pound dried black beans, soaked
3 quarts water or chicken stock
1 pound ham hock
3 cloves garlic, minced
2 onions, chopped
1/2 cup chopped celery
1/2 cup chopped tomatoes

1/2 cup minced parsley
1/4 teaspoon cloves
1 tablespoon Worcestershire
1/4 cup sherry (optional)
Chopped boiled egg
Lemon slices

Place all ingredients (except sherry, egg, and lemon slices) in large stockpot. Bring to boil, turn to simmer, and cook for 4 hours. Add sherry. Serve with sprinkles of chopped egg and lemon slices. A spoon of cooked rice may be added before filling bowl. Serves 6-8.

STRING BEAN SOUP

1 (16-ounce) can French-style
  green beans
1 medium onion, finely chopped
1 medium potato, cubed

2 cups chicken broth
1/2 cup cream
Salt and pepper to taste
Croutons

Drain beans; cut through beans several times. Add onions and potatoes. Bring chicken stock to boil. Add vegetables, salt and pepper. Turn to simmer. Cook until potatoes are tender but not mushy. Add cream, heat several minutes. Pour into soup bowls. Garnish with croutons. Serves 4.

LENTIL STEW

8 cups vegetable stock
1 cup dried lentils
1 large sweet red pepper, cut into narrow (1-inch) strips
6 scallions, sliced
3 medium carrots, sliced

1 small zucchini, sliced
2 medium tomatoes, diced
1 tablespoon Tamari or soy sauce
1/4 teaspoon oregano
1/4 teaspoon rosemary

Place stock and lentils in a stockpot over medium heat and bring to boil. Add pepper, scallions, carrots, zucchini, tomatoes, soy sauce, oregano, and rosemary. Bring to boil. Cover, reduce heat, and simmer for 45 minutes. Serve hot. Makes 6 servings.

LENTIL SOUP WITH FRANKFURTERS

2 quarts beef broth
1 1/2 cups lentils, rinsed
1 ham bone
2 ribs celery, sliced
2 carrots, sliced
1 teaspoon salt

1/2 teaspoon pepper
2 tablespoons minced parsley
2 tablespoons butter
2 medium onions, sliced thin
6 frankfurters, cut diagonally in 1/2-inch slices

Place broth in kettle. Add lentils, ham bone, celery, carrots, salt, pepper, and parsley. Bring to boil, cover, lower heat. Simmer for 2 hours until lentils are tender.

Remove from heat. Remove ham bone. Force mixture through coarse sieve. Return to kettle. Heat butter in skillet. Add onions and frankfurters. Cook over low heat, stirring until onions are tender and franks are lightly brown; add to soup mix. Cook 10 minutes or until soup is hot. Serves 6-8.

To build a digestive tolerance to beans, eat them regularly.

PEA POD SOUP

7 tablespoons butter (reserve 1
  tablespoon)
3/4 cup onion, chopped
3/4 cup green onion,
  chopped
3 tablespoons flour
1 tablespoon sugar
1 bay leaf
1 teaspoon white pepper

1/4 teaspoon fresh ground
  nutmeg
Salt to taste
4 cups chicken broth
1 package frozen green peas
1 cup fresh Chinese pea pods
2 egg yolks
1 cup heavy cream

In 3-quart heavy saucepan, sauté onions in 6 tablespoons butter; add flour and stir. Add sugar, bay leaf, pepper, nutmeg, and salt. Stir in chicken stock. Bring to boil; simmer 15 minutes. Add frozen peas; cook 3 minutes. Remove bay leaf. Pour mixture in blender. Return to heat. Sauté pea pods in remaining butter; add purée. Beat egg yolks and cream; gradually add to soup. Adjust seasoning. Serves 6.

RICH PEANUT SOUP

1 stick butter
1 medium onion, finely chopped
1 rib celery, finely chopped
1 tablespoon plain flour
4 cups chicken stock
1 1/2 cups creamy peanut butter

Salt and pepper to taste
Juice of one lemon
2 cups half-and-half or cream
Lemon slices dusted with parsley
  (garnish)

Melt butter in large saucepan; add onion and celery and cook mixture until onion is transparent—10 minutes. Add flour; blend well. Add chicken stock. Bring to boil until thick and smooth. Reduce heat; simmer 20 minutes.

Remove vegetables with slotted spoon. Stir in peanut butter; add salt, pepper, lemon juice and cream. Simmer 5-10 minutes. Serve with lemon slices as garnish. Serves 8.

SOUTHERN DINER PEANUT SOUP

A tradition of diners on southern trains, especially those leaving Washington traveling south. This simple soup was a standard.

3 cups milk
3/4 cup creamy peanut butter
1 teaspoon Worcestershire

1/8 teaspoon each chili powder, cayenne, and Tabasco

Gradually stir milk into peanut butter in 2-quart saucepan. Cook over low heat until hot. Add seasonings. Mix well. Serves 4.

TEX-MEX CHILI WITH BEANS

1/4 cup vegetable oil
2 medium onions, chopped
3 garlic cloves, minced
1 pound beef, cubed, (1-inch
   squares)
2 (16-ounce) cans tomatoes
1 cup water
1/2 cup chili powder
1 tablespoon sugar

1 tablespoon sugar
1 teaspoon red pepper
2 teaspoons salt
1 teaspoon cumin
4 cups cooked kidney beans
Jalapeño pepper, seeded,
   chopped

In large pot heat oil, add onions, garlic; sauté until onions are tender. Add beef and cook until meat is browned. Drain fat. Add all ingredients except beans and jalapeños. Simmer beef mixture 1 1/2 to 2 hours. Add beans; cook 30 minutes. Add pepper to taste. Serves 8-10.

Adjust seasoning simply means to salt or pepper to your individual or family taste.

REAL CHILI

2 cups dried pinto beans
1 pound lean beef, cut in
   1/2-inch cubes
2 tablespoons oil
1 large onion, chopped
3 cans tomatoes, drained,
   reserve liquid

1 cup beef stock or broth
2 cloves garlic, minced
1 teaspoon cumin
1 tablespoon salt

Soak beans overnight or use hot-soak method: boil 5 minutes, set for 1 hour. Rinse beans after soaking. Cover with fresh water in large saucepan. Cook 1 hour until almost tender. Set aside.

Brown beef in heated oil until lightly brown. Add onions. Drain tomatoes, purée in blender, add to beef mixture. Add stock, garlic, cumin and salt. Use reserved tomato juice as chili cooks down. Drain beans and add to tomatoes and beef mixture. Let chili sit to blend flavors. Reheat and serve. Serves 4.

Note: Grated Cheddar cheese and minced green onions are excellent garnishes for chili.

CAPITOL HILL BEAN SOUP

Legislated to permanently be on the menu of both dining halls.

SENATE

2 pounds Michigan navy beans
1 1/2 pounds smoked ham hocks
1 medium onion

1 tablespoon butter
Salt and pepper to taste

HOUSE

Omit onions from ingredients

Wash beans and run through hot water until beans turn white. Place in 4-quart container with water to cover. Add ham hocks and bring to a boil. Lower heat to medium and cook for 3 hours. Keep pot covered during cooking. Braise onion in hot butter until tender; add to soup. Remove ham hocks and cool. Remove meat and return diced to pot. Add salt and pepper. Just before serving, bruise a portion of the beans with large spoon, enough to cloud liquid. Serves 6. Refrigerate leftovers promptly.

30

PINTO BEAN GUMBO

1 2/3 cups dry pinto beans	2 cups fresh okra, cut
or dry navy beans	2 cups whole kernel corn,
7 cups water	drained
1 large onion, chopped	2 cups canned tomatoes, cut
1/2 cup diced salt pork	1 teaspoon each: thyme, sugar,
1/2 teaspoon salt	Worcestershire sauce
1 bay leaf	Hot sauce to taste

Soak beans overnight or use quick soak method. Do not drain. Add onion, salt pork, salt, bay leaf. Bring to boil, then reduce to simmer and cook 2 to 2 1/2 hours. Add remaining ingredients. Simmer until okra is tender, about 30 minutes. Remove bay leaf. Adjust seasoning. Serves 8-10.

PEANUT SAUCES AND DRESSINGS

The wonders of this legume never cease—one of the most versatile of the pea pod family.

PEANUT SAUCE: (for chicken, pork, or white navy beans)

1/2 cup chicken broth	1/2 cup milk
4 tablespoons peanut butter	1 teaspoon each soy sauce,
1/2 teaspoon garlic salt	sugar, and red pepper

Mix all ingredients in medium saucepan. Cook over low heat, stirring frequently until sauce thickens, 3-4 minutes. Makes 1 cup.

GINGERED PEANUT SAUCE: (for green beans, green peas, broccoli)
An Oriental taste adapted from daughter-in-law Adele's recipes.

1/2 cup chunky-style peanut butter	1 tablespoon soy sauce
1/2 cup water	1 clove minced garlic
1/2 cup white vinegar	1 teaspoon ground ginger

Beat peanut butter with water and vinegar. Add remaining ingredients. Heat to serve over vegetables, or stir into hot vegetables the last 5 minutes of cooking.

    Variation for green beans: To above recipe add 4 tablespoons sherry and substitute 1/2 teaspoon curry powder for ginger.

PEANUT BARBECUE SAUCE FOR VENISON

1/2 cup butter	2 tablespoons smooth peanut
2 teaspoons celery seed	butter
Salt to taste	3/4 cup vinegar
1 teaspoon pepper	2 teaspoons lime juice

Melt butter in saucepan. Add celery seed, salt, and pepper. Heat until blended. Stir in peanut butter, vinegar, and lime juice. Cook over low heat 5-10 minutes, stirring constantly. Pass to spoon over venison or beef. Makes about 1 1/2 cups.

BLACK BEAN SAUCE FOR FISH

Spoon this spicy sauce over fish fillets before baking or broiling. Fine French cooks use this extensively.

2 tablespoons soy sauce	1/4 teaspoon sugar
2 tablespoons white wine	Salt and pepper to taste
1 teaspoon olive oil or peanut oil	1/2 cup cooked black beans,
1/2 teaspoon chopped fresh ginger	minced

Mix all ingredients together in small saucepan. Heat 3-5 minutes. Spoon warm sauce over fish fillets just before serving. Makes enough sauce for 4 fish servings.

LENTIL SPAGHETTI SAUCE

2 tablespoons olive oil	1/2 teaspoon crushed basil
(or vegetable oil)	1 teaspoon dry oregano
1 medium onion, chopped	1 teaspoon white sugar
4 cloves garlic, minced	1 bay leaf
1 cup fresh mushrooms, sliced	1/2 teaspoon salt
8 ounces tomato sauce	1/8 teaspoon pepper
4 ounces tomato paste	12 ounces spaghetti, cooked,
2 1/3 cups water	drained
1/2 cup lentils, washed	

Sauté onion, garlic, and mushrooms in oil until onion is soft. Add remaining ingredients except spaghetti. Bring to a boil. Reduce heat, cover and let simmer on low heat for 30-40 minutes. Serve over spaghetti (angel hair is my favorite in this recipe) cooked al dente. Serves 6.

GARBANZO SAUCE FOR SPAGHETTI
A vegetarian delight.

3 cups canned garbanzos
  (do not drain)
2 tablespoons olive oil
1 medium onion, chopped
2 cloves garlic, minced
1 (16-ounce) can tomatoes,
  drained and mashed

2 tablespoons fresh parsley,
  minced
Ground pepper to taste
1 pound spaghetti, cooked,
  drained
Grated Parmesan cheese

Purée garbanzo beans. Set aside. Heat oil; sauté onions and garlic until onions are tender. Add tomatoes, parsley, and pepper to onions. Heat 10 minutes. Add puréed beans to tomato mixture. Cook an additional 10 minutes. Serve on spaghetti. Garnish with Parmesan cheese. Serves 6-8.

BLACK BEAN SAUCE FOR BEEF OR PORK

2 tablespoons vegetable oil
2 cloves garlic, minced
1/4 cup cooked black beans,
  mashed
1 teaspoon white wine

1/2 teaspoon sugar
1 tablespoon dark soy sauce
2 teaspoons cornstarch
1/2 cup water

Heat oil. Add garlic; sauté 1 minute. Add beans and stir-fry an additional minute. Add wine, sugar, and soy sauce. Gradually stir in cornstarch to 1/2 cup water. Add to bean mixture; stir constantly to blend mixture. Serve hot over meat. Makes 1 cup.

A savory is several herbs and spices tied together and removed from the bean pot after cooking is completed.

MIXED BEAN RELISH

A perfect accompaniment served cold with meat dish—hamburger, pork loin, or beef roast.

2 cups shredded cabbage	2 cups cooked, cut green beans
2 green tomatoes, seeded, chopped	1 tablespoon celery seed
2 cups sliced celery	3 cups cider vinegar
1 red pepper, seeded, cut in strips	2 tablespoons mustard seed
1 green pepper, seeded, cut in strips	2 cups water
1 medium white onion, cut in rings	1 cup sugar
2 cups cooked lima beans	1 tablespoon salt

In large bowl, combine cabbage, tomatoes, celery, peppers, and onion. Cover with salted water (1/4 cup salt per quart of water), let stand overnight.

Drain and rinse well. Combine celery seed, vinegar and mustard seed; mix with limas, green beans, and all seasonings in large pan. Add water, sugar, and salt. Bring to boil and cook 10 minutes. Pack in hot jars, leaving 1/2-inch space at top. Seal. Process 5 minutes in boiling water. Cool. Store. Makes 4 pints.

ITALIAN BEAN SAUCE FOR PASTA

A short three-word reference to a bean sauce eaten at a restaurant near Rome led to this creation.

2 cups cooked navy beans	1 cup low-fat yogurt
(prepared from dried beans)	Salt and fresh-ground pepper
1/4 cup virgin olive oil	to taste

Blend all ingredients in food processor or blender until mixture is smooth and creamy. Thin with additional yogurt if necessary. Heat; toss through pasta.

The natural buttery taste of beans like navy or limas does not need flavor. Salt, pepper, and a little onion will suffice.

MISSOURI SWEET PEPPER RELISH
FOR WHITE BEANS

Lambert's Restaurant in Sikeston, Missouri, is famous for its 'throwed rolls' and pots of white beans. The owner kindly shared the recipe and a nice lady in St. Louis relayed the quantities for the relish that is passed with the beans.

18 fresh, firm tomatoes, chopped
  into small pieces
4 large red sweet peppers,
  finely chopped
4 medium onions, finely chopped
1/3 cup salt

2 1/2 cups sugar
3 cups cider vinegar
3 tablespoons whole mustard
  seed
1/2 tablespoons celery seed
2 teaspoons paprika

Mix tomatoes, peppers, onions, and salt, and refrigerator overnight. Bring sugar, vinegar, mustard seed, celery seed, and paprika to a boil in medium pan. Simmer for 5 minutes. Stir in tomato mix. Pack in hot, sterile jars. Makes 4 quarts.

SALADS

WINE DRESSING FOR BEAN SALADS

2 tablespoons vermouth
2 tablespoons wine vinegar
2 garlic cloves, crushed
1/2 teaspoon dry mustard

2 tablespoons mustard or dill
   seed
1/2 teaspoon brown sugar
3/4 cup vegetable oil

Blend ingredients in pint bottle. Chill. Shake well before using with fresh green beans, limas, peas, or cooked dried beans.

GREEN BEAN SALAD

2 (16-ounce) cans green beans
Water (lightly salted)
2 tablespoons sugar
1/2 cup olive oil

1/2 teaspoon salt
1/2 teaspoon celery salt
1/2 teaspoon paprika

Cook beans in lightly salted water 5 minutes. Drain. Mix remaining ingredients. Marinate in refrigerator for several hours. Before serving, add the following:

1/2 cucumber, sliced thin
1 medium red onion sliced and
   made into rings

1/2 cup diagonal-cut celery
2 teaspoons pimento

Serves 6-8.

Variation: Add 1 cup diced boiled potatoes and 1/2 cup vinegar.

MARINATED BEAN SALAD

2 (16-ounce) cans French-style
  green beans
1 (16-ounce) can baby lima beans
1 (16-ounce) can tiny green peas
1 (14-ounce) jar pimento, chopped
4 ribs celery, chopped
1 large purple onion, chopped

1 large green pepper, chopped
1 cup sugar
1 cup salad oil
1 cup vinegar
Salt and pepper to taste
6-7 garlic cloves

Drain all vegetables. Combine first 7 ingredients. Sprinkle mixture
with sugar. Add oil and vinegar. Stir well and add salt and pepper
to taste. Insert toothpicks into 6 or 7 cloves of garlic and put into
salad. Cover; refrigerate overnight. Remove garlic cloves; stir and
serve. Serves 12.

BEAN SALAD WITH TUNA

1 (16-ounce) can great northern
  beans or pinto beans, drained
1 (9 1/3-ounce) can tuna, drained,
  flaked
1/4 cup sliced ripe olives

1/2 teaspoon salt
3 tablespoons minced parsley
1/2 cup finely chopped celery
3 tablespoons white wine
3 tablespoons onion

Mix beans, tuna and olives. In jar with top, mix remaining ingredients. Chill, then drizzle over bean mix. Serves 6.

BEAN SALAD IN POCKET BREAD

2 cups cooked, drained pinto
  beans
3 hard-cooked eggs, chopped
1/2 cup chopped sweet pickles
2 tablespoons chopped onion

1/2 teaspoon salt
4 tablespoons mayonnaise
5 pocket bread rounds, cut in
  half
Chopped lettuce

Mash beans until smooth, add eggs, pickles, onions, salt, and mayonnaise. Chill 1-2 hours. Spoon about 2 tablespoons of bean mixture into each pocket. Top with chopped lettuce. Serves 5.

GREEK GARBANZO BEANS WITH ANCHOVY

Take a little food trip to Greece with this dish—use as salad or vegetable.

2 cups cooked, drained garbanzo
  beans (chickpeas)
1 can anchovy fillets, soaked in
  milk, chopped
1/4 cup black or green olives,
  pitted, minced
2 tablespoons lemon juice

1 garlic clove, minced
6 tablespoons olive oil
Salt and pepper to taste
4 slices red onion, divided into
  rings (garnish)
Minced fresh parsley for garnish

Mix garbanzo beans, anchovies, and olives in serving bowl. Mix lemon juice, garlic, oil, and salt and pepper. Combine dressing with beans. Let stand at room temperature several hours for flavors to blend. Garnish with onion rings and parsley. Serves 4-6.

BEAN TACO SALAD

2 cups cooked kidney beans,
  drained
1 small onion, chopped
2 fresh tomatoes, diced
1 large avocado, peeled, chopped
1/2 cup diced stuffed green olives
1 cup shredded Cheddar cheese

1 cup French dressing
1 tablespoon brown sugar
1 tablespoon vinegar
1 small head iceberg lettuce,
  chopped
2 cups corn chips

In large salad bowl, mix beans, onion, tomatoes, avocado, olives and grated cheese. Blend French dressing with sugar and vinegar. Lightly toss dressing into salad mix. Mix lettuce and corn chips into bean mix. Serves 8.

Beans take longer to cook at high altitudes unless you use a pressure cooker to help speed the process.

BLACK-EYED PEA SALAD

6 ounces slab bacon, chopped
3/4 cup walnut pieces
2 (10-ounce) packages frozen
    black-eyed peas, cooked, drained
2 red bell peppers, diced
1 medium zucchini, cut lengthwise
    into quarters, sliced

1/4 cup minced fresh parsley
1/3 cup olive oil
2 tablespoons red wine vinegar
2 tablespoons Dijon mustard
1 clove garlic, minced
Salt and freshly ground pepper

Fry bacon in medium skillet until crisp; drain on paper towel. Add nuts to skillet and cook, stirring constantly, until toasted. Transfer to paper towel. Combine warm peas, bacon, and walnuts in mixing bowl. Add bell peppers, zucchini, and fresh parsley, and toss to combine. Whisk together oil, vinegar, mustard, garlic, salt and pepper to taste; add to salad and toss well. Serve on platter lined with lettuce. Serves 6.

KIDNEY BEAN SALAD

1/4 cup vegetable oil
Juice of one lemon
1/4 teaspoon dried dill
1/4 teaspoon dried mint leaves
1 tablespoon chopped parsley
1/4 teaspoon salt

1/8 teaspoon pepper
1 (20-ounce) can kidney beans,
    drained, washed
4 green onions, chopped
Sliced boiled egg (garnish)
Sliced tomato (garnish)

Beat oil and lemon juice. Crush dill and mint with back of spoon before adding to oil mixture. Add parsley, salt and pepper. Mix seasoned oil with beans and onions. Chill overnight. Garnish with quartered eggs and tomatoes. Serves 4-6.

BAYOU BEAN SALAD

1 (16-ounce) can French-style
    green beans
1 (16-ounce) can English peas
1/2 cup shredded red cabbage

1/2 cup sliced celery
1 (4-ounce) jar drained pimentos
1 medium red onion, sliced,
    separated into rings

DRESSING:
1 cup red wine vinegar
1/2 cup olive oil
1 cup brown sugar

4 tablespoons water
1/4 teaspoon paprika
Salt to taste

Mix well, drained beans and peas. Blend dressing ingredients. Pour over bean mixture. Cover and marinate overnight. When ready to serve, drain beans saving marinade. Add cabbage, celery, and pimentos. Lightly toss in onion rings. Add enough marinade to bind ingredients. Serves 10.

WHITE BEAN SALAD

1 cup dried navy beans, chickpeas, or lima beans
1/2 cup chopped onion
2 garlic cloves, minced
1/4 cup minced fresh parsley

3/4 cup red wine vinegar
1/2 teaspoon salt
1/3 cup olive oil or salad oil
1/4 teaspoon pepper
1/8 teaspoon oregano

Soak beans overnight in enough water to cover. Drain well. Cover with fresh water. Bring to boil, reduce heat and simmer 1 hour until beans are tender. Drain, rinse under cold water (use colander); transfer to serving bowl. Blend remaining ingredients thoroughly. Pour over beans, tossing carefully not to bruise beans. Chill overnight. Serves 6-8.

GREEN PEA PASTA SALAD PRIMAVERA

1 cup green split peas, rinsed and drained
4 cups water
8 ounces cooked corkscrew or other small pasta
1/4 cup white wine vinegar
1 garlic clove, minced
1 tablespoon Dijon mustard
1/4 teaspoon crushed red pepper flakes

1/2 teaspoon salt
1/4 teaspoon pepper
2 tablespoons olive oil
1 1/2 cups diced red or green pepper
1 1/2 cups thinly sliced green onion

In saucepan, combine peas and water. Cover; bring to boil. Reduce heat; simmer covered 12-15 minutes or until peas are just tender. Drain. Cook pasta according to package directions.

Meanwhile, combine vinegar, garlic, mustard, red pepper, salt and pepper. Beat in oil. Add remaining ingredients and peas; toss. Chill. Serves 8-10 (8 cups).

ORANGE-PEA SALAD

2 (10-ounce) packages frozen
  peas
1 1/3 cups chopped celery
2 tablespoons chopped fresh mint
  or 1/2 teaspoon dried leaf
  tarragon
1/4 cup sour cream
2 teaspoons grated orange rind

2 tablespoons frozen
  concentrated orange juice,
  thawed, undiluted
1/2 teaspoon sugar
1 teaspoon salt
Salad greens
1 orange, sectioned

Cook peas according to package directions. Drain and cool. Mix with celery, mint, sour cream, orange rind, concentrated orange juice, sugar and salt. Chill. Turn into bowl lined with salad greens and garnish with orange sections. Serves 6.

EASY SWEET PEA SALAD

1 (17-ounce) can sweet peas
2 hard-boiled eggs, diced
3 tablespoons chopped onions
2 tablespoons chopped pimento

1/4 cup mayonnaise
1/2 teaspoon salt
1 teaspoon vinegar
Black pepper, as desired

Drain peas and add remainder of the ingredients. Cover and chill 1 hour. Stir again and serve. Serves 4-6.

CRUNCHY GREEN PEA SALAD

1 package frozen green peas,
  thawed
1 green pepper, cut in strips
2 ribs celery, chopped
1 red onion, chopped
2 teaspoons sesame seeds

1/2 cup Spanish peanuts
1/2 cup sour cream
1 tablespoon lemon juice
1/2 teaspoon paprika
1/4 teaspoon rosemary
Boiled egg for garnish

Mix peas, pepper, celery, onions, sesame seeds, and peanuts. Blend sour cream, lemon juice, paprika and rosemary. Lightly mix pea mixture with sour cream mixture. Serve on lettuce leaf; garnish with quartered egg slices. Makes 4-6 servings.

FIESTA PEA SALAD

1 cup green split peas, rinsed and drained
4 cups water
1/4 cup wine vinegar
1 clove garlic, minced
1 tablespoon Dijon mustard
1/4 teaspoon crushed red pepper flakes

Salt and pepper to taste
1/4 cup salad oil
2 tablespoons olive oil
4 cups cooked rainbow rotini
1 cup diced red pepper
1 cup diced red onion
2 small tomatoes, wedged

In saucepan, combine peas and water. Cover; bring to a boil. Reduce heat; simmer 10-15 minutes or until peas are just tender but firm. Drain and cool peas. Meanwhile, combine vinegar, garlic, mustard, red pepper flakes, salt and pepper. Beat in oils. Combine cooled peas with cooked pasta, red pepper, and red onion. Carefully stir in dressing. Chill. Just before serving, garnish with tomato wedges. Serves 8.

BROCCOLI-LENTIL SALAD

1 cup lentils, rinsed
2 cups water
1 teaspoon salt
1/8 teaspoon pepper
1/2 cup Ranch-Style dressing

1 cup chopped celery
1/2 cup chopped green onions
1 cup chopped jicama (optional)
2 cups chopped broccoli

Bring to boil lentils and water. Cover and simmer 15 minutes. Drain. While hot, add salt, pepper and prepared Ranch-Style dressing made with buttermilk. Place in refrigerator to chill. When chilled, add chopped vegetables. May need to add some additional salt, pepper, and dressing. Serves 10.

Spices and herbs are an excellent substitute for salt and are a tasty alternative for those requiring a low sodium diet.

LENTIL CONFETTI SALAD

1/2 cup lentils, rinsed and drained
1 1/2 cups water
1 teaspoon salt
1 cup cooked rice
1/2 cup Italian salad dressing
1 small tomato, diced

1/4 cup chopped green pepper
1/4 cup chopped onion
1 tablespoon each chopped celery
    and sliced, pimento-stuffed
    olives

In saucepan, combine lentils, water, and salt. Cover; bring to a boil. Reduce heat; simmer 20 minutes or until lentils are tender. Drain. Meanwhile, in a bowl, combine remaining ingredients. Add lentils; toss. Chill. Serves 6 (2 1/2 cups).

CURRIED LENTIL RICE SALAD

Lentils + rice = complete protein, so this savory salad makes a substantial main dish. The cool and creamy yogurt dressing adds extra flavor and nutrition.

1 cup lentils
2 cups water
1 cup plain yogurt
2 tablespoons lemon juice
2 tablespoons chopped fresh mint
1 tablespoon curry powder
2 cloves garlic, minced
Dash freshly ground pepper

1 cup cooked rice
1 medium cucumber, peeled,
    seeded and sliced thin
1 cup chopped sweet red or
    green pepper
1 cup chopped green onion
Salt and pepper to taste

Wash and pick over lentils. Place in medium saucepan with 2 cups water. Heat to boiling, cover, reduce heat and simmer 10-12 minutes or just until lentils are barely tender. Drain, if necessary. Combine yogurt, lemon juice, mint, and seasonings. Add to lentils along with all remaining ingredients. Cover and chill several hours to blend flavors. Serves 6.

LIMA BEAN SALAD

1 cup cooked baby lima beans,
    drained and rinsed
1/2 cup celery, cut fine
1/2 cup chopped green onions
1/4 cup chopped green pepper
1/4 cup pimento

2 tablespoons fresh minced
    parsley
1/4 cup olive oil
1/4 cup white vinegar
Salt and pepper to taste
Lettuce leaves

Mix limas, celery, onions, pepper, pimento, and parsley. Blend olive oil, vinegar, salt and pepper. Toss with bean mix. Serve on lettuce leaves. Serves 4-6.

HERBED LENTIL AND RICE SALAD

1 cup lentils
1 tablespoon crab boil seasoning
    mix
2 cups water
1 cup cooked brown rice
1 cup chopped green pepper
1/2 cup chopped green onion
1/2 cup chopped fresh parsley

1 teaspoon grated lemon peel
1/3 cup lemon juice
1/4 cup olive or salad oil
1 tablespoon chopped fresh
    marjoram or 1 teaspoon dried
    marjoram leaves, crumbled
Salt and pepper to taste

Wash and pick over lentils. Place in medium saucepan with crab boil mix and 2 cups water. Heat to boiling, cover, reduce heat, and simmer 10-12 minutes or just until lentils are barely tender. Drain if necessary. Combine with remaining ingredients.and chill several hours or overnight to blend flavors. Serve with an array of fresh sliced fruits or vegetables or on fresh spinach or other greens. Serves 4-6.

Substitute cooked beans, cup for cup, in a poultry stuffing, using beans in place of bread.

LIMA BEAN-TOMATO SALAD

2 cups shelled fresh lima beans
8 medium tomatoes
1 tablespoon chopped fresh
  parsley
1 small onion, grated

1/4 cup finely chopped celery
1/4 teaspoon freshly ground
  pepper
1/2 cup Italian reduced-calorie
  salad dressing

Cook lima beans, covered, in boiling water to cover 15-20 minutes or until tender. Drain and set aside to cool. Cut off top of each tomato; scoop out pulp, leaving shells intact. Invert shells on paper towels to drain; chop pulp. Combine tomato pulp, lima beans, and remaining ingredients; toss gently. Fill tomato shells with bean mixture and chill. Serves 8.

BAKED BEANS

It was hard to decide just how many baked bean recipes to include in this book, because baked beans are as all-American as hamburgers, hot dogs, and apple pie. The following recipes represent a number of regional variations of the classic dish. Enjoy!

OLD-FASHIONED BAKED BEANS

2 (16-ounce) cans pork and beans
1 tablespoon mustard
1/4 cup brown molasses
2 teaspoons salt
1 medium green pepper, chopped
1 large onion, chopped

2 tablespoons sweet pickle relish
1/2 cup catsup
1/2 teaspoon pepper
1/2 teaspoon ground cinnamon
4 slices bacon

Combine all ingredients except bacon. Pour into buttered 9x13-inch baking dish. Place bacon slices on top. Bake in slow oven, 300 degrees, for 2 hours. Serves 6-8.

NEW ENGLAND BAKED BEANS

1 cup dried navy beans
1/2 teaspoon salt
1 medium onion, chopped
2 tablespoons olive oil
2 garlic cloves, minced
1 tablespoon dry basil

1 tablespoon dried parsley
1/4 cup dark molasses
1/4 cup honey
1 tablespoon Dijon mustard
1/4 teaspoon cayenne pepper

Soak beans overnight. Drain and wash 3 times. Place beans in a large pot or Dutch oven. Cover with water. Do not salt until near end of cooking time. Cook until beans are tender, 1 1/2 to 2 hours on simmer. Add remaining ingredients. Place in large Pyrex baking dish. Bake in slow oven, 325 degrees, for 2 hours. Serves 6-8.

BARBECUED BAKED BEANS

3 slices bacon	1/2 cup barbecue sauce
1 medium onion, chopped	2 tablespoons brown sugar
1 medium green pepper, chopped	3 tablespoons vinegar
2 (16-ounce) cans baked beans	1/2 teaspoon prepared mustard
1 (15-ounce) can kidney beans	1/4 teaspoon pepper
1 (16-ounce) can lima beans	

In medium skillet, cook bacon until crisp. Crumble and set aside. Drain fat except for about 2 tablespoons. Reheat drippings, add onion and pepper, and cook until onions are tender. Mix together onions, bacon, and all remaining ingredients. Pour into large baking casserole (2 1/2 to 3 quarts). Bake uncovered in 350-degree oven for 1 hour. Yields 8-10 servings.

DELTA BAKED BEANS

3 (# 2 1/2) cans pork and beans	1/2 cup chili sauce
1 large onion, chopped	1/2 cup tomato catsup
6 cloves garlic, minced	1/4 cup molasses
4 tablespoons mustard seed	1/4 cup water
2 tablespoons brown sugar	

Mix all ingredients together; place in large (2-quart) baking dish. Bake in slow oven, 250 degrees, 3-4 hours. Add small amount of water if beans become too dry. Serves 12.

BOSTON BAKED BEANS WITH MAPLE SYRUP

1 1/2 cups white navy beans	2 tablespoons dark molasses
1 teaspoon salt	1/4 pound salt pork, diced
1 teaspoon baking soda	1 teaspoon rosemary or 2
1 teaspoon prepared mustard	fresh sprigs
2 tablespoons pure maple syrup	

Soak beans overnight or by quick-soak method (see Peas in the Pot) in 6 cups of water. In same water, add remaining ingredients to beans. Stir to mix well. Pour in large casserole. Bake in very slow oven (275 degrees) for 6 hours. Serves 6.

BAKED BEANS WITH PLUM PRESERVES

Bean lovers with a sweet tooth will fall in love with this quick bean bake.

2 tablespoons butter
2 medium onions, sliced thin
1/4 cup plum preserves
1 teaspoon thyme
6 slices fried bacon, crumbled

1 (18-ounce) can baked beans
1 teaspoon dry mustard
1/4 teaspoon fresh ground
pepper

In large, heavy skillet, heat butter; add onions and cook, stirring, until onions are soft. Move aside. Place preserves in skillet. Stir until melted. Stir onions and preserves together; cook 3-5 minutes. Add remaining ingredients. Simmer on top of stove on low heat 20 minutes until heated through. Serves 4-6.

BAKED BEANS FOR A CROWD
(A crowd meaning 10, maybe 12 hungry people.)

2 sticks butter or margarine
2 green peppers, sliced
3 onions, chopped
2 small cans mushrooms,
bits and pieces
1 pound country sausage or
pepperoni, sliced thinly
4 bacon slices, cut in
small pieces
4 eggs, boiled and chopped
2 cans whole tomatoes, mashed

1 teaspoon chili powder
1 tablespoon Worcestershire
sauce
1 cup dark molasses
Jalapeño peppers to taste
(optional)
4 (16-ounce) cans barbecued
beans
2 cups grated cheese of choice
(Swiss, Cheddar)

In a large skillet, melt butter, add peppers, onions, mushrooms, meat, and bacon bits. Cook over high heat until onions are tender. Add eggs, tomatoes, chili powder, Worcestershire sauce, molasses, and sliced peppers. Mix this cooked mixture with beans. Pour in 1 very large or 2 medium baking dishes. Cover with grated cheese. Bake in 325-degree oven for 2 hours. Serves 10-12.

49

SPICY BAKED BEANS

2 (16-ounce) cans pork and beans
1/2 cup brown sugar
1 tablespoon Worcestershire sauce
1/4 teaspoon pepper
1 teaspoon salt
4 cups chopped onion
1 cup chopped green peppers

2 garlic cloves, minced
1/4 teaspoon oregano
1/4 teaspoon cumin
1 cup tomato sauce
1/4 cup chili sauce
4 slices bacon

Combine all ingredients except bacon. Pour into large baking dish. Lay strips of bacon across top. Cover with foil. Bake at 325 degrees for 2 1/2 to 3 hours. Serves 8.

SPIKED BAKED BEANS

1 cup onions, chopped
1 cup celery, chopped
1 cup green pepper, chopped
3 tablespoons butter
1 cup whiskey

2 (16-ounce) cans pork and beans
2 tablespoons prepared mustard
1 cup barbecue sauce
1 cup brown sugar

Sauté onions, celery, and green pepper in butter. Combine ingredients; bake 1 hour at 325 degrees. (Whiskey evaporates.) Serves 8.

PICNIC BAKED BEANS

Make these ahead. Reheat and carry in insulated container to picnic site—YUM!

2 pounds dried great northern
   or navy beans
2 garlic cloves, chopped
2 medium onions, chopped
1 bay leaf
6 whole cloves
8 slices bacon, chopped

2 cups minced onion
2 cups brown sugar
1/2 cup dark molasses
1/2 cup cider vinegar
1/4 cup prepared mustard
1 teaspoon salt
1/4 teaspoon pepper

In large saucepan, place beans in boiling water to cover. Let stand several hours. Add garlic, chopped onion, bay leaf, and cloves. Place over medium heat and cook until beans are tender, 1 1/2 to 2 hours. Reserve liquid. In bean pot or Dutch oven, fry bacon pieces until brown. Remove most of fat. Add onions and cook until tender. Add sugar, molasses, vinegar, mustard, salt and pepper. Drain beans and add to onion mixture. Add bean juice if too dry. Bake 3-4 hours in 325-degree oven. Serves 10-20.

BAKED BEANS 5 A.M.

Great for outdoors or indoors before going outdoors!

1 (28-ounce) can pork and beans   **4 slices bacon**
4 eggs   **1 cup grated Cheddar cheese**

Empty beans into medium-size baking dish. Make four 'nests' and break eggs into beans. Cover each with slice of bacon. Sprinkle with cheese. Bake in 375-degree oven for 15-20 minutes. Serves 4.

BEAN POT

1 (#2) can pork and beans   **1 clove garlic, chopped**
1 (#2) can kidney beans   **1/2 cup catsup**
1 (#2) can green beans   **1 teaspoon mustard**
1 onion, chopped   **1/4 cup brown sugar**
1 green pepper, chopped   **4 slices bacon, minced**

Combine all ingredients and mix well. Place in large baking dish. Bake 1 hour at 350 degrees. Makes 8-10 servings.

Use leftover baked beans as a stuffing for baked onion shells. Great side dish.

MAIN DISHES

AND

SIDE DISHES

CLASSIC RED BEANS AND RICE

1 pound red beans	1/4 cup olive oil
(soaked several hours)	1 ham hock
1 pound andouille or link sausage	Hot sauce to taste
2 large onions, chopped	2 bay leaves
1 large green pepper, chopped	Rice
2 cloves garlic, chopped	

Rinse beans and place in large pot with water to cover. Dice sausage in 1/2-inch rounds. Add remaining ingredients to beans except rice. Bring to a boil for 10 minutes, then turn heat to medium. Cook minimum of 2 hours, adding more water if beans cook down too much. Remove bay leaves and ham hock before serving over fluffy rice.

CLASSIC BOILED RICE:

1 cup rice	1 teaspoon olive oil
3 1/2 cups water	1 teaspoon salt

Bring water to a boil; add rice, salt, and olive oil. Boil on reduced heat 10-15 minutes. Rinse and drain rice in colander. Add 1/2 cup water to pot and bring to a boil. Place colander over water to steam, covered, before serving. Serves 8-10.

SPICY RED BEANS AND RICE

1 pound dried red beans	1 cup parsley, chopped
2 quarts water	1 tablespoon salt
1/2 pound salt pork or ham hock	3/4 teaspoon red pepper
3 cups chopped onion	1 teaspoon black pepper
1 bunch green onions with tops, chopped	1/4 teaspoon oregano
	2 bay leaves
1 cup chopped green pepper	3-4 generous dashes of Tabasco
2 large cloves garlic, crushed	1 tablespoon Worcestershire sauce

Cover beans with water and soak overnight, or 2-3 hours. Drain and cook beans in 2 quarts of water for 45 minutes. Add remaining ingredients and cook slowly for 2-3 hours, stirring occasionally. Serve over boiled rice. Serves 4-6.

LOUISIANA RED BEANS

In south Louisiana, these are affectionately called Cooney Beans.

1 pound dried red kidney beans	3 garlic cloves, whole
4 onions, chopped	1 teaspoon pepper
1/2 pound salt pork	Red pepper pods, to taste
2 bay leaves	

Soak beans overnight. Drain. Place in 3-quart pot and add remaining ingredients. Bring to a boil, then turn to simmer and cook 2-3 hours. Remove pepper pods, bay leaves and garlic cloves. Serve with fresh French bread. Serves 6-8.

Cooking beans an extended time causes loss of flavor. Near the end of the cooking time, you may need to adjust the flavors.

AUTHENTIC RED BEANS AND RICE

Although dried or canned kidney beans have become accepted in recipes, the dark-red round bean is the authentic bean for this classic southern dish.

1 pound dried red beans	1/2 teaspoon dried thyme
3 quarts water	1/4 dried red chili pepper
1/4 pound salt pork or ham hock	Salt and pepper to taste
2 medium onions, chopped	Cooked rice
2 ribs celery, cut	Parsley to garnish or chopped
2 bay leaves	green onions

Wash beans carefully. Bring 1 1/2 quarts water to boil; add beans, boil for 5 minutes. Remove from heat and soak for 1 hour. Drain beans and set aside. Add 1 1/2 quarts fresh water to pot. Add salt pork, onions, celery, bay leaves, thyme, and chili pepper. Boil 15-20 minutes to season stock. Add red beans; simmer until beans are tender (1 to 1 1/2 hours.) Discard pork and bay leaves. Serve over cooked rice. Garnish with choice of parsley or onions. Serves 8-10.

AUTHOR'S FAVORITE RED BEANS AND RICE

This 'top of the beans' recipe came to me from daughter-in-law, Cindy, via a friend. Do not be dismayed by the amount of onions! They don't even 'show' once the beans cook.

1 pound dried red beans	1 pound andouille sausage or
6 onions, chopped coarsely	link sausage
2 pods garlic, chopped	Dash Tabasco
2 bay leaves	Pepper to taste
1/4 pound salt pork	Water to cover
1/4 pound real butter (1 stick)	(No salt needed)

Place all ingredients in large, heavy saucepan, 4 to 6-quart size. Cover with water. Bring to a boil, then turn to medium low and simmer 4-6 hours. Add water if beans get too dry. You do not soak beans for this recipe. They cook tender with slow cooking. Serve with Classic Rice. Serves 8-10.

MEATY RED BEANS AND RICE

1 pound dried red beans
1/2 pound cubed ham
(1/2-inch thick)
1 pound link sausage, sliced
1 pound hot bulk sausage
1 medium green pepper, chopped

3 large onions, chopped
3 garlic cloves, minced
1 teaspoon black pepper
1/4 teaspoon chili powder
1 teaspoon salt
1/2 teaspoon cumin

Soak beans overnight. Drain. Place beans and all ingredients in large (4-quart) pot. Cover with water. Bring to a boil. Reduce and simmer 2-3 hours. Beans will remain whole on slow simmer. To thicken beans, remove 1/2 cup, mash and return to mixture. Serve over hot rice. Serves 6-8.

RED BEAN SUPPER DISH

Buttered corn bread squares and a simple green salad will make this a complete meal.

1/2 pound red kidney beans
(dried)
1/2 pound small red beans
(dried)
6 cups water
2 tablespoons butter
1 cup chopped green onions
1 cup chopped yellow onions
2 ribs celery, chopped
2 cloves garlic, minced
2 large meaty ham hocks,
cracked

4 chicken bouillon cubes
4 beef bouillon cubes
1/2 teaspoon black pepper
1 teaspoon prepared mustard
1/2 teaspoon Tabasco sauce
1 (15-ounce) can seasoned
tomatoes, drained
2 tablespoons honey or brown
sugar
Juice of half a fresh lemon

Place beans in large boiling pot with 6 cups of water. Bring to a boil for 5 minutes. Set aside for 1 hour, with lid off. Heat 2 tablespoons butter in skillet and sauté onions, garlic, and celery until onions are limp. After an hour, place beans in colander over pot to drain, saving liquid. Measure the liquid to make 4 cups, adding water if necessary, and return to the cooking pot with vegetables. Add beans, ham hocks, beef and chicken cubes, and pepper. Bring to a boil, turn to simmer, and cook beans 2 hours adjusting flavors in last half hour. Chop drained tomatoes. Ad,d tomatoes, mustard, Tabasco, sugar or honey, and lemon juice to pot. Heat thoroughly. Remove ham hocks, removing meat and returning to pot. May be served with rice and garnished with chopped green onions. Serves 8-10.

CHILI CON LENTILS

5 cups water
1 (16-ounce) can chickpeas,
  drained
1 cup chopped onion
1/2 cup chopped celery
1 large clove garlic, minced
2 teaspoons ground cumin
1 teaspoon salt
1 pound (2 1/3 cups) lentils,
  rinsed and drained

1 (16-ounce) can kidney beans,
  drained
1 (16-ounce) can tomatoes,
  cut-up
1/2 cup chopped carrot
1/2 cup chopped green pepper
1 tablespoon chili powder
1 teaspoon crushed red pepper
  flakes

In a large heavy pot, combine all ingredients. Cover; bring to a boil. Reduce heat; simmer 30 minutes or until lentils are tender. Top with shredded Cheddar cheese. Makes 11 cups.

RED LENTIL-VEGETABLE STIR-FRY

1 cup red lentils, rinsed and
  drained
2 1/2 cups water
1 teaspoon vinegar
1/4 teaspoon salt
2 cups sliced zucchini squash

1 cup sliced fresh mushrooms
1 cup coarsely chopped onion
2 garlic cloves, minced
1/2 teaspoon each crushed
  basil and rosemary leaves
1/4 cup butter or margarine

In 2-quart saucepan, combine lentils, water, vinegar, and salt. Cover; bring to a boil. Remove from heat. Let stand 5 minutes. Rinse with cold water. Meanwhile, in skillet, cook zucchini, mushrooms, onion and garlic with basil and rosemary in butter until tender. Add lentils. Heat; stir occasionally. Serve hot or cold. Serves 6.

One cup cooked dried beans plus one serving of rice, grain, eggs, cheese, or nuts equals the 15 grams of protein found in a 2-ounce sirloin steak.

57

CURRIED LENTILS FROM INDIA
The name for this traditional dish is DAL!

4 cups water
2 cups dried lentils, red or
  yellow
1 teaspoon curry powder
1/2 teaspoon salt
1/2 cup butter
1/2 cup chopped onions

1 teaspoon cumin
1 large tomato, chopped
  coarsely
3 tablespoons cream
Chopped cashew nuts for
  garnish (optional)

In large saucepan bring water to boil. Add lentils, curry, and salt.
Cook covered until water is absorbed and lentils are tender, about
30 minutes. Melt butter in skillet over low heat. Add onions and
sauté till tender. Add cumin, tomatoes. Cook 2 minutes. Stir in
cream. Place lentils in serving bowl. Spoon tomato mixture over
top. Garnish with chopped cashew nuts. Serves 6.

LENTIL PATTIES

1 cup lentils, rinsed and
  drained
2 cups water
1/2 cup finely chopped onion
3/4 cup sunflower seeds
1 egg, slightly beaten

1/3 cup fine dry bread crumbs
1/4 cup chopped pecans
1/4 cup chili sauce
2 tablespoons butter or
  margarine
Yogurt

In saucepan, combine lentils and water. Cover; bring to a boil.
Reduce heat; simmer 30 minutes or until lentils are tender. Drain.
In a bowl, with a fork or potato masher, mash lentils. Add onion,
sunflower seeds, egg, bread crumbs, pecans, and chili sauce. Mix
thoroughly. Shape into 6 patties. In a skillet, melt butter. Add patties. Cook on medium heat until brown on each side and heated
through. Serve with yogurt. Serves 6.

---

*Lentils cook very quickly. Do not stir during cooking or you will bruise
the peas.*

58

LENTIL PILAF

1 bunch green onions, chopped
1-2 cloves garlic, minced
1/4 cup wild rice, washed
1/2 cup white long grain rice
1 cup lentils, washed
1/4 cup butter

2 3/4 cups chicken broth
1/2 teaspoon thyme
1/2 teaspoon salt
1/8 teaspoon pepper
1 ounce slivered almonds

Sauté the onion, garlic, rice, and lentils in butter until onion is tender (about 3-4 minutes). Add the rest of the ingredients and bring to a boil. Reduce heat; cover. Simmer 30 minutes or until all the water is absorbed. Serves 6.

CHICKPEA CASSEROLE

2 tablespoons oil
2 medium onions, chopped
4 cups canned chickpeas, drained
1 cup whole tomatoes, drained
1 (6-ounce) can tomato paste
1 cup water

1 teaspoon coriander
1 teaspoon cumin
3 tablespoons parsley flakes
Seasoned bread crumbs
2 tablespoons butter

Heat oil in skillet. Add onions and sauté until tender. Drain. Mix together with peas, tomatoes, tomato paste, water, and seasonings. Place in buttered casserole. Sprinkle with bread crumbs; dot with butter. Bake at 350 degrees for 30 minutes. Serves 6.

QUICK AND SPICY CHICKPEAS

1 clove garlic, peeled and minced
1 onion, peeled and chopped
1 tablespoon oil
1 tablespoon grated fresh ginger

1 tablespoon curry powder
1 (28 ounce) can tomatoes,
   chopped, including juice
3 (1-pound) cans chickpeas

Combine garlic, onion, oil, and ginger in large, deep skillet. Cook about 4 minutes over medium-high heat. Add curry powder and cook, stirring, another minute. Add tomatoes and chickpeas and cover. Cook 10 minutes, stirring occasionally until heated through. Serves 8-10.

TRADITIONAL BEAN CASSOULET

A true cassoulet has at least 2 meats and sausage and simmers for 2 or 3 days on the back of the stove, but this version can be managed in a couple of hours with precooked meats.

1 pound courtry sausage, cut in
 2-inch slices
1 bottle dry white wine
1 pound country ham slices,
 cut bite-size
1 large onion, chopped
2 cloves garlic, minced
2 cups chopped tomatoes, fresh
 or canned

1 bay leaf
Pepper to taste
1/2 teaspoon basil
2 teaspoons sugar
1 pound dried lima or butter
 beans, soaked overnight
1/4 cup chicken broth or bouillon
5 tablespoons parsley

Place sausage in large frying pan or saucepan. Pour wine to cover half of sausage. Cover. Bring to boil and steam 15 minutes. Remove cover. Sauté sausage until brown. Add ham pieces and additional wine if needed. Simmer 5 minutes. Add onion, garlic, tomatoes, bay leaf, pepper, basil and sugar. Cook 10 minutes and add beans, chicken broth, parsley, and remaining wine. Liquid should cover beans; if not, add water. Cover and cook 1 1/2 to 2 hours until beans are tender, adding water when necessary. Adjust salt and pepper seasonings. Serves 8.

COWBOY BEER BEANS

2 pounds pinto beans
1 (12-ounce) bottle beer
1 1/2 to 2 pounds lean slab bacon
 cut into 1-inch cubes, or 2 or
 3 ham hocks
2 medium onions, chopped
1 bell pepper, seeded, diced
2 or 3 garlic cloves, minced

1 (16-ounce) can whole tomatoes,
 cut up
2 jalapeños, sliced
1 tablespoon chili powder
1 teaspoon black pepper
1/2 teaspoon red pepper
Salt to taste (after beans are
 cooked)

Soak the beans overnight; drain off the soak water. (If you don't have time to soak, cover the beans with water, bring to a boil, simmer 2 minutes, remove from heat, cover, let stand an hour, drain.) Put beans in a Dutch oven. Pour in beer and enough water to come up 2 inches over the beans. Add remaining ingredients except salt. Cover, bring to a boil, reduce heat, and simmer for 5-6 hours over very low heat—just enough to bubble the liquid a little. Add salt to taste when the beans are cooked. Serves 12-15.

OLE-FASHION BLACK-EYED PEAS

2 cups dried black-eyed peas
5 cups water
1 pound ham hock

1 medium onion, chopped
1 teaspoon salt
1 minced garlic clove

Sort and wash peas; place in large Dutch oven. Cover with water
and let soak 3-4 hours. Drain. Return to pot and cover with 5 cups
water and remaining ingredients. Bring to boil; simmer 1 hour until peas are tender. Serves 8.

Variation: Add 1/2 cup chopped green pepper, 1 bay leaf, and 1
can stewed tomatoes.

SPICED BLACK-EYED PEAS

1 (1-pound) package dried
  black-eyed peas (cooked
  according to package
  instructions)
1 cup chopped green pepper
1 cup chopped onion
4-6 jalapeño peppers, chopped

1 teaspoon salt
1 teaspoon ground pepper
1/2 teaspoon each cinnamon,
  ginger, and nutmeg
1/2 cup tomato paste
1 (16-ounce) can tomatoes
Hot sauce to taste

To pot of cooked black-eyed peas, add all the remaining ingredients. Cook on medium heat 45 minutes, adding small amounts of
water if necessary and adjusting seasoning or salt. Serves 10-12.

BLACK-EYED PEA PATTIES

Tastes like a real meat pattie. Honest!

2 cups cooked black-eyed peas,
  drained and rinsed
1 large onion, finely chopped

3 tablespoons plain flour
Salt and pepper to taste
Oil for deep-fat frying

Mash peas thoroughly. Add onion and seasoned flour, blending
well. Heat oil in heavy skillet. Fry until brown on both sides.
Makes 4-6 patties.

---

*The southern tradition of eating beans for luck centers around the beans
representing coins. Turnip greens represent folding money.*

BLACK-EYED PEAS AND TOMATOES

Many black-eyed pea eaters chop their tomatoes and onion on top of the cooked peas—and often the peas are on top of crumbled hot corn bread. Fine for those who like it mess-kit fashion—but this recipe seems a little more genteel.

3 cups fresh shelled black-eyed
  peas
1 ham hock

1 small onion, finely chopped
3 fresh tomatoes, chopped
Salt and pepper to taste

Place fresh peas in 4-quart pot with water to cover. Add ham hock and onions. Bring to boil, turn to simmer, and cook for about an hour. Add tomatoes, salt, and pepper, and cook until peas are tender. A dash of Tabasco may be added before serving. Serves 6.

Note: Cooked dried peas or canned may be substituted for fresh.

BLACK-EYED PEAS WITH SALSA

An old standby with a new twist of taste.

1 pound dried black-eyed peas
1/2 pound salt pork, diced
4 garlic cloves, minced
1 large onion, sliced thin
2 bay leaves

1 dried red pepper
1/2 cup dark molasses
1 stick butter, melted
Salsa

Cook peas in boiling water for 1 hour. In same water, add diced pork, garlic, onion, bay leaves, pepper, molasses, and butter. Cook over low heat until peas are tender, approximately 1 additional hour. Drain, remove bay leaf, pepper, and pork. Transfer peas to large buttered casserole. Add Salsa and bake 20 minutes in moderate 350-degree oven.

SALSA:

2 cups chopped fresh tomatoes
1 cup chopped green onion
  (1 bunch)
1/4 teaspoon coriander
2 jalapeño peppers, seeded and
  diced
1 teaspoon cumin

1 teaspoon oregano
1 tablespoon olive oil
1 tablespoon lemon juice
1 teaspoon salt; pepper to taste
1/2 teaspoon sugar
Cayenne pepper to taste

Mix all ingredients, blending thoroughly before mixing with peas. Serves 6.

HOPPIN' JOHN

1 pound dried black-eyed peas,
  washed and picked over
8 1/2 cups water, divided
1/2 pound smoked hog jowl or
  ham hock
1 onion, sliced

1 pod hot red pepper or 1/2
  teaspoon bottled liquid hot
  red pepper sauce
1/4 teaspoon salt
1 cup regular rice

Place peas in a large pot and add 6 cups of water. Let soak overnight. The next day, add hog jowl or ham hock, onion and red pepper. Bring to a boil. Reduce heat and cook, uncovered, until the peas and meat are tender, about 1 1/4 hours.

Remove from heat. Remove pepper pod. In another saucepan, heat remaining 2 1/2 cups water with the salt. When it comes to a boil, add rice. Reduce heat and cook, covered, until rice is tender and all liquid has been absorbed, about 20 minutes. Meanwhile, remove any skin and bones from the jowl or ham hock and cut the meat into small pieces. Return meat to the pot. Add rice to the pot with the peas and heat through. Makes 10 servings.

CROCKPOT RED BEANS

4 tablespoons steak sauce
2 tablespoons Worcestershire
  sauce
3 (16-ounce) cans red kidney
  beans

1 pound smoked sausage, cubed
2 large onions, chopped
Tabasco to taste

Place sauces on bottom of crockpot. Layer beans, sausage and onions. Sprinkle each layer with Tabasco sauce. Cook on low 3 hours. Serve over cooked rice. Serves 8.

Add 1/2 teaspoon ginger to beans during cooking or soaking to help prevent discomfort in digestion of dried beans.

CHILI PIE WITH BEANS

3 tablespoons olive oil
1 clove garlic, finely chopped
1 medium onion, chopped
1 pound boneless beef round,
1/2-inch cubes
2 bay leaves
1 green pepper, chopped
2 whole red chilies, seeded

2 cups beef bouillon
1 cup red wine, divided
2 cups cooked kidney beans,
drained
1 teaspoon each ground cumin,
oregano, paprika, coriander,
pepper, thyme, pepper,
and sugar

In 3 to 4-quart saucepan, heat oil. Add garlic, onion and beef cubes. Cook 3 minutes until beef is browned. Add bay leaves, pepper and chilies. Cook 1 minute. Add bouillon and one-half of wine. Cook several minutes to blend ingredients. Pour into 4-quart size bake-and-serve casserole and cover. Bake in 350-degree oven 45-60 minutes, until beef is tender. Discard chilies. Mix spices and seasonings into beans. Stir into beef mixture. Cover with cornbread topping. Bake 20 minutes until cornbread is done. Serves 6-8.

CORN BREAD TOPPING:

1 cup cornmeal
1/2 cup flour
1 teaspoon salt
2 teaspoons baking powder

3/4 cup milk
1 egg
2 tablespoons oil
1 cup shredded Cheddar cheese

Mix all dry ingredients. Fold in milk, egg and oil. Mix well. Stir in cheese.

REFRIED BEANS

1 large onion, chopped
2 cloves garlic, crushed
4 tablespoons butter
2 (16-ounce) cans refried beans

1/2 cup chopped tomatoes
1 (4-ounce) can jalapeño relish
8 ounces sharp Cheddar cheese

Sauté onions and garlic in butter until soft. Stir in refried beans; add tomatoes and relish, and heat thoroughly. Add cheese, stirring until melted. Serves 6-8.

REFRIED BEANS IN CORNMEAL CRÊPES

Great on a cold night for a filling supper. Add a salad and fresh fruit for a complete protein meal.

2/3 cup cornmeal	1 cup skim milk
1/2 cup plain flour	4 tablespoons corn oil
1/4 teaspoon salt	1-2 (16-ounce) cans refried
2 eggs	beans

Mix all ingredients except oil and beans and beat until smooth. Allow to stand 30 minutes at room temperature before cooking crêpes. Heat oil in 7-inch crêpe pan or similar frying pan. When oil is hot, pour 3 tablespoons of batter into pan and rotate until the batter covers the surface. When the edges are beginning to crisp and brown, turn crêpe with spatula. Heat for a few seconds, then turn onto a warm plate. Without adding oil, continue to make crêpes. Keep batter thin. Keep crêpes warm.

Spoon hot refried beans on one-half of crêpe. Roll and place seam side down in an appropriate dish. May be reheated in microwave 1 minute on high or in standard hot oven for 10 minutes. Serves 4-6.

RED BEANS BOURGUIGNON

2 tablespoons butter	2 fresh medium tomatoes,
3 medium onions, chopped	peeled and quartered
2 (13-ounce) cans red kidney beans	1/4 teaspoon garlic salt
1 cup burgundy wine	1 teaspoon parsley flakes
1 teaspoon Worcestershire sauce	Salt and pepper to taste
1/2 large green pepper, chopped	

Heat butter in small skillet and brown onions. Drain. Add to beans and remaining ingredients. Place in bean pot or large casserole dish. Bake 45 minutes, covered, in 325-degree oven. Serves 6-8.

Simmer beans covered to keep skins from breaking.

BEAN CHALUPAS

2 cups dried pinto beans
5 cups water
2 cloves garlic, minced
1 (4-ounce) can chopped green
  chilies, drained
1/2 cup chopped onion
2 tablespoons chili powder
2 teaspoons ground cumin
1 1/2 teaspoons salt
1 teaspoon dried whole oregano

Vegetable oil
8 (6-inch) corn tortillas
Shredded lettuce
3/4 cup (3 ounces) shredded
  Monterey Jack cheese
3/4 cup (3 ounces) shredded
  Cheddar cheese
1/2 cup sliced ripe olives
1/2 cup commercial sour cream
4 tomatoes, cut into wedges

Sort and wash beans; place in a large Dutch oven. Cover with water 2 inches above beans; let soak overnight. Drain beans. Add 5 cups water and next 7 ingredients. Bring to boil; cover, reduce heat, and simmer 1 1/2 hours. Remove 1 cup of beans, and place in container of electric blender; process until smooth. Stir puréed beans into bean mixture; cover and simmer 30 minutes. Uncover and simmer an additional 30 minutes.

Heat 2 inches of oil in a large skillet to 350 degrees. Fry 1 tortilla about 5 seconds to soften; press tortilla into oil with a round, flat potato masher, molding tortilla into a bowl shape. (Use a wooden spoon if necessary to shape sides.) Drain well on paper towels. Repeat process with the remaining tortillas. Spoon an equal amount of bean mixture into each tortilla; place on a bed of lettuce. Sprinkle with cheese and olives; top with a dollop of sour cream. Garnish with tomatoes. Yields 8 servings.

SAVORY PINTO BEANS

1 pound pinto beans
2 onions, chopped
1 green pepper, finely chopped
Jalapeños to taste
3 fresh tomatoes, chopped
1/2 teaspoon pepper

1/2 teaspoon cumin
1/2 teaspoon oregano
2 bay leaves
2 garlic cloves, minced
1/2 cup coarsely chopped celery

Wash beans carefully. Place in 4-quart container with water to cover. Add remaining ingredients except celery. Bring to a boil, turn to medium heat and cook 3-5 hours until beans are tender. Add celery and cook an additional 30 minutes. Serves 6-8.

COWBOY POT ROAST WITH BEANS

1/2 cup dry kidney beans
1/2 cup pinto beans
1/2 cup great northern beans
3 cups hot water
1 tablespoon vegetable oil

3-4 pound pot roast
2 garlic cloves, chopped
1 cup chili sauce
2 celery stalks, cut in chunks
1 chopped onion

Cover beans with water and soak overnight. Heat 1 tablespoon oil in heavy skillet to brown pot roast. Remove from pan. Drain excess oil. Drain beans. Rinse twice. Cover bottom of 13x9x2-inch Pyrex casserole dish with beans. Mix remaining ingredients and place on top of beans. Center pot roast on top. Cover with foil. Bake at 350 degrees approximately 2 1/2 hours. Serves 6-8.

MOCK SAUSAGE

1 cup dried lima beans or 3 cups
  cooked limas
3 eggs, divided
1/2 teaspoon sage

Salt and pepper to taste
2/3 cup bread crumbs
2 tablespoons vegetable oil

Wash dried beans, cover with water, and soak overnight. Drain. Cook in salted boiling water until tender, about 1 hour. Drain and press through a strainer. Add 2 beaten eggs, sage, salt and pepper. Form into patties. Roll in crumbs, then 1 beaten egg, then crumbs again. Sauté in hot oil until brown. Serve with heated tomato sauce. Serves 4-6.

Less is more. Never mask your basic dish with seasoning. Do lots of tasting and a little adding at a time.

BARBECUED LIMAS

1 1/2 cups large dried lima beans
  or great northern beans
3 1/2 cups water
1 1/2 teaspoons salt
4 strips bacon
1 medium onion, chopped

1 clove garlic, minced
1 can tomato soup
1 tablespoon vinegar
1 tablespoon prepared mustard
1 teaspoon chili powder
1 teaspoon Worcestershire sauce

Wash beans. Cover with water and soak overnight or bring to boil
and let sit for several hours. Add salt; bring to boil. Reduce heat
and simmer beans until barely tender (1 1/2 to 2 hours). Drain, re-
serving 1/2 cup liquid.

In medium skillet, cook bacon partially done. Set aside. Drain
all but 1 tablespoon of fat. Sauté onion and garlic, then add all ingredients except bacon. Heat to boiling. Add beans. Stir to blend;
turn into 1-quart baking dish. Top with partially cooked bacon.
Bake at 350 degrees for 1 hour. Serves 6.

*triple recipe fills both the large + sm
brown pyrex dishes). Will be very thin
after 1 hr but OK - (they really thicken)
after cooling*

LIMA BEAN ROAST

1 cup roasted shelled peanuts
2 cups seasoned mashed potatoes
2 cups cooked lima beans, fresh
  or canned
1/4 cup milk

1 egg, well beaten
1 teaspoon salt
1/8 teaspoon paprika
1 teaspoon onion juice

Grind peanuts, using finest blade of processor or food chopper.
Grease a medium-size baking dish. Begin with potatoes, then layer
beans and peanuts. Blend milk with egg and seasonings. Pour over
top and bake in moderate oven (350 degrees) until brown (15-20
minutes). Serves 6.

---

*Store dried beans in a glass jar in a cool pantry or the refrigerator; they
will keep for a year.*

LIMA BEAN CURRY

1 pound dried lima beans	1 teaspoon cumin
2 teaspoons salt	1 teaspoon coriander
2 tablespoons butter	1 cup fresh tomatoes, diced,
1 medium onion, finely chopped	seeded
2 cloves garlic, minced	1 green chili pepper, seeded
2 teaspoons ginger	Juice of 1 lemon
1 teaspoon curry	

Soak beans overnight. Drain. Cover with water in large saucepan. Add salt. Bring to a boil, turn to medium heat, and cook beans until tender, about 1 1/2 hours. Drain. Reserve juice.

Heat butter in large saucepan; add onion and garlic and sauté onion until tender. Add remaining ingredients, stirring over medium heat 5 minutes. Add 1 1/2 cups of liquid to tomato mixture. Cook until mixture thickens. Add beans and cook additional 10 minutes. Serve over rice. Serves 6.

SPANISH BAKED LIMA BEANS

1 pound dried lima beans	6 tablespoons vegetable oil
(large or medium)	1 1/2 tablespoons chili powder
3 teaspoons salt	1 1/2 tablespoons cornstarch
1 1/2 cups chopped onion	1 1/2 cups cold water
1 1/2 cups chopped green pepper	1 1/2 cups grated Cheddar
1 clove garlic, minced	cheese

Soak beans overnight. Drain. Cover with salted water and cook 45 minutes. Sauté onion, green pepper, and garlic in oil until golden. Mix chili powder, cornstarch, and water until smooth. Add to sautéed vegetables and cook 3 minutes. Combine with drained beans and 1 cup grated cheese. Place in 2-quart casserole and sprinkle with remaining cheese. Bake uncovered at 350 degrees for 30 minutes. Serves 6-8.

Nutritionally, dry peas and lentils are a complex carbohydrate.

CARAMELED LIMA BEANS

1 pound large dry lima beans
1 1/2 cups granulated sugar
1/2 stick butter

1/4 cup flour
3 tablespoons white vinegar
Salt to taste

Cover lima beans with water. Bring to a boil, then turn to simmer. Cook until beans are tender, approximately 1 1/2 hours.

In small skillet, brown sugar with butter until light in color. Blend flour, vinegar, and 1 cup of water from drained beans. Simmer 1 minute. Place beans in serving bowl and pour caramel mixture over top. Serves 4-6.

BLACK BEANS IN WINE

2 cups black beans
2 quarts water
1 pound salt pork, cut in
    small pieces
1 cup chopped onion

2 cloves garlic, minced
1/2 tablespoon oregano
1 bay leaf
1/2 cup red wine
2 tablespoons olive oil

Wash beans thoroughly, cover with 2 quarts warm water. Soak for 3 hours. Bring to boil, then simmer until tender, 1-2 hours. Fry salt pork until crisp. Drain. Sauté onions and garlic in hot pot until tender. Add oregano, bay leaf, salt pork pieces, red wine and olive oil. Mix with beans. Simmer on low another hour. Serves 6-8.

CALIFORNIA BLACK BEANS AND RICE

1 pound black beans
1 cup smoked ham, cubed
Salt and pepper to taste,
1 cup olive oil

1 large onion, chopped
3 cloves garlic
1 medium green pepper, chopped
2 tablespoons vinegar

Wash black beans, discarding ones that rise to top. Place in 4-quart pot. Cover with water. Bring to boil, turn to simmer and cook for 1 1/2 hours. Add ham, salt and pepper to taste. Heat oil; sauté onion, garlic, and pepper until tender. Drain. Add to beans. Cook additional half hour; add vinegar. Serve on rice. Garnish with sliced eggs or minced green onion. Serves 6-8.

ITALIAN CANNELLINI BEANS

This white kidney bean dish is like a trip to Rome.

1 tablespoon olive oil
1 small onion, chopped
2 cloves garlic, minced
2 (20-ounce) cans cannellini beans
  (white kidney), drained
1 (16-ounce) can tomatoes

4 ounces pepperoni, chopped
1/2 teaspoon dried basil, crushed
1/2 teaspoon oregano
1/8 teaspoon red pepper
1 cup provolone cheese, shredded

In medium skillet heat oil; sauté onions and garlic until onions are tender. Mix together beans, tomatoes, pepperoni, and seasonings. Add onion mix. Turn beans into 2-quart casserole. Bake, uncovered, in 300-degree oven 45 minutes. Sprinkle with cheese. Heat until cheese melts (5 minutes). Serves 8.

WHITE BEANS FLORENCE

1 pound great northern
  white beans
1/4 pound salt pork
2 tablespoons olive oil
2 onions, chopped

3 cloves garlic, minced
1 (16-ounce) can tomatoes,
  drained
1 teaspoon sage
Salt and pepper to taste

Wash beans, drain; add fresh water to cover. Bring pot to boil. Remove from heat and let beans stand 1 hour. Drain beans of soaking water, add fresh water to cover and salt pork. Cook on medium heat approximately an hour, until beans are becoming tender.

In large saucepan heat olive oil, add onions and garlic. Sauté until onions are limp. Add tomatoes to mixture, stirring to break up pieces. Stir in sage and salt and pepper to taste. Let sauce thicken slightly, drain beans, and add to tomato mixture. Continue cooking until beans are very tender, usually a half hour. Serves 6.

Substitute chopped cooked beans for meat in a lasagna recipe.

WHITE BEANS PROVENÇAL

1 pound white dried beans
1 1/2 tablespoons thyme
1 1/2 cups dry white wine
1/4 cup butter or margarine
2 tablespoons olive oil
1 small onion, chopped
1 garlic clove, crushed
1 (12-ounce) can whole tomatoes,
    undrained

2 bay leaves
10 small white boiling onions
Salt and pepper to taste
3 carrots, peeled and diced
2 cups sliced zucchini, sliced
12 pitted ripe olives
Minced fresh parsley for garnish

Wash dried beans. Cover with water and soak overnight. Drain, add white wine, thyme, and fresh water to cover. Cook over medium heat until beans are tender, 1 1/2 to 2 hours.

Mix butter and olive oil, heat in large skillet and sauté onions and garlic until golden brown. Add tomatoes, bay leaves and boiling onions. Simmer 1 hour. Add salt, pepper and carrots. Cook approximately 30 minutes until carrots are tender. Add zucchini and olives. Cook an additional 10 minutes. Sprinkle parsley on top. Serves 8-10.

BRANDIED NAVY BEANS

1 pound navy beans
1 ham hock
1 (1-pound) can tomatoes
1 (4-ounce) can tomato paste
2 onions, chopped
1/2 teaspoon chili powder
Red pepper to taste

1 tablespoon brown sugar
1 tablespoon A-1 sauce
1 tablespoon Worcestershire
    sauce
1 teaspoon parsley flakes
1 teaspoon Savory Salt
1/4 cup brandy

Soak beans overnight. Drain. Place in large pot with ham hock and water to cover. Bring to boil. Simmer for 1 hour. Drain, discard ham hock. Make tomato sauce, mixing remaining ingredients in order. Place in greased casserole. Bake at 200 degrees for 6 hours. If more liquid is needed, add brandy and water. Serves 8-10.

FRESH GREEN PEA PIE

When I discovered this recipe, it was an unexpected gift because of its uniqueness. Try it soon.

Butter pastry for 2-crust pie
3 cups fresh (or frozen) green peas (3 pounds)
1 teaspoon sugar
1 stick butter
2 tablespoons fresh minced parsley

Salt and pepper (white preferred) to taste
1 bouillon cube dissolved in 1/4 cup water
1 tablespoon cream

Prepare pastry. Refrigerate until needed. Place peas in 4 cups salted boiling water. Add sugar and cook 15-20 minutes until peas are tender, but still bright green. Drain peas of cooking water. Add butter, parsley, salt and pepper, and chicken broth. Allow to cool. Peas should be moist for filling.

Prepare 2 pastries for crust. Place circle to loosely fit 9-inch pie pan. Spoon peas into pie shell. Cover with second pastry round. Crimp edges. Slash top to allow steam to escape. Brush top crust with cream. Place in preheated 400-degree oven, on lower rack. Bake 25-30 minutes, until rich brown. Cool 5 minutes before cutting. Serves 6-8.

STIR-FRIED PEA PODS WITH SHRIMP

3 tablespoons corn oil
1/2 teaspoon ground ginger
1 clove garlic, minced
1 1/2 pounds uncooked shelled, deveined shrimp
1/2 pound fresh pea pods or 1 (6-ounce) package frozen

1/2 cup drained bamboo shoots
1/4 cup chicken bouillon
1 tablespoon soy sauce
1 tablespoon dry white wine
1 teaspoon sugar

Heat oil in wok or large skillet; add ginger, garlic, and shrimp. Stir fry until shrimp turns pink, about 2 minutes. Add pea pods, bamboo shoots, bouillon, soy sauce, wine and sugar. Stir fry 2 minutes. Serve over hot cooked rice. Serves 4.

Variation: In place of shrimp, substitute 1 to 1 1/4 pounds of scallops. Add a dash of cayenne pepper to seasonings.

CHINESE PEA PODS

Quickly done—impressive to guests.

1 tablespoon salad oil
1 clove garlic, minced
1 (10-ounce) can bamboo shoots,
 drained
1 (8-ounce) can water chestnuts,
 drained, sliced
1 can mushrooms, drained
2 thin slices ginger root
2 cups Chinese pea pods, fresh
 or frozen

1 tablespoon soy sauce
1 chicken bouillon cube
 dissolved in 1/4 cup water
1/2 teaspoon sugar
2 teaspoons cornstarch in
 2 tablespoons cold water
Slivered almonds for garnish

In large skillet or wok, heat oil, add garlic, bamboo shoots, water chestnuts, mushrooms, ginger root, pea pods, and soy sauce. Stir fry 1-2 minutes. Add bouillon and sugar. Simmer 2 minutes. Add cornstarch-water mixture, and stir 1-2 minutes until thickened. Garnish with slivered almonds. Serves 6.

TAIWAN PEAS

1/2 cup water
1 chicken bouillon cube
1/4 teaspoon ginger
1 teaspoon sugar
1 tablespoon oil
1 (5-ounce) can water chestnuts,
 sliced

1 can mushrooms, drained
1 package frozen green peas
1 1/2 teaspoons cornstarch
1 tablespoon soy sauce

In 2-quart saucepan, place water, bouillon, ginger, sugar, and oil. Add water chestnuts, mushrooms, and peas. Bring to boil, turn to simmer for 10 minutes. Mix cornstarch and soy sauce, stir gently into pea mixture until thickened. Serves 4-6.

SPLIT PEA PATTIES

1/3 cup dry split peas
2 cups chicken broth
1 small onion, diced
1 carrot, shredded
1/2 cup flour
1 teaspoon baking powder

1/8 teaspoon each salt
 and pepper
1/4 cup milk
1 egg, beaten
1 tablespoon oil

In 2-quart saucepan, combine peas, chicken broth, onion, and carrot and bring to a boil. Cook covered until peas are soft, about 30 minutes. Cool. Mix flour, baking powder, salt and pepper. Add milk and egg to split pea mixture, mixing well. Add pea mixture to flour mixture. Heat oil in skillet. Spoon tablespoon-size fritters into hot oil. Brown on both sides. Repeat process to make 12 fritters. Serve with white sauce or sour cream.

SPLIT PEA BAKE

1/4 cup butter or margarine,
  divided
1 medium onion, chopped
2 cups cooked split peas
2 cups boiled rice

2 cups canned tomatoes,
  drained
Salt and pepper to taste
1/2 cup bread crumbs

Heat 1 tablespoon of butter in small skillet. Sauté onion until tender. Drain. Layer peas, rice, tomatoes, and onions in greased baking dish. Season with salt and pepper. Cover with bread crumbs. Dot with remaining butter. Bake 20 minutes in hot 375-degree oven. Serves 6-8.

BAKED PEANUT LOAF

2 tablespoons vegetable oil
2 tablespoons chopped onion
2 tablespoons minced celery
2 tablespoons chopped green
  pepper
1 1/2 cups coarse crushed
  peanuts

1 cup bread crumbs
1 cup mashed canned green
  beans
2 tablespoons lemon juice
1 teaspoon salt
Pepper to taste
1 egg, slightly beaten

Heat oil, cook onion, celery, and pepper until tender. Drain. Mix all ingredients, adding egg last. Pack in greased loaf pan. Bake in 350-degree oven. Serve with a white cream sauce, garnished with minced green parsley. Serves 4-6.

Variation: Add 1 cup shredded carrots.

PEANUT SCRAPPLE

1 quart boiling water
1 cup hot milk
1 cup yellow cornmeal
3/4 cup hominy grits
1 1/4 teaspoons salt
1/8 teaspoon paprika

1/4 to 1 cup grated Cheddar
 cheese
1 3/4 cups chopped peanuts
1 egg, beaten
1 cup bread crumbs

Combine hot water and milk in 2-quart saucepan. Bring milk mixture to a boil, gradually stir in cornmeal and grits with salt and paprika added last. Cook until mixture begins to thicken. Place in double boiler. Add cheese and peanuts. Cook on medium heat 1 hour. Slice, dip in beaten egg, then bread crumbs to coat. Fry in deep fat, browning on each side. Serve with heated Peanut Sauce (see page 32). Serves 6.

BEEF, BEANS, AND MACARONI CHILI

1/2 pound ground beef
1 small onion, chopped
2 cups canned tomatoes
 (save liquid)
1 3/4 cups cooked kidney
 beans (save liquid)

2 teaspoons chili powder
3/4 cup uncooked elbow
 macaroni

Fry beef and onion to light brown; drain fat. Chop tomatoes. Add enough water to tomato and bean liquid to equal 1 cup. Add tomatoes, beans, liquid, chili powder, and macaroni to bean mix. Bring to boil, then simmer covered 20 minutes until macaroni is tender. Stir occasionally. Add water if necessary. Serves 4.

Variation: Add red pepper, cayenne, or Tabasco for more flavor.

TAILGATE CHILI

And don't forget the chocolate—wait and see.

4 tablespoons vegetable oil
4 medium onions, chopped
2 garlic cloves, diced
2 tablespoons each powdered
 cumin, oregano, and coriander
6 cans drained canned tomatoes
 (3 cups)

2 cups water
2 squares unsweetened chocolate
2 tablespoons vegetable oil
2 pounds cubed lean beef
2 cans drained kidney beans
Salt to taste

Heat oil in large kettle, cook onions and garlic until soft; add seasonings, tomatoes, and water. Simmer 10-20 minutes; add chocolate.

Heat oil in another skillet; brown beef. Drain. Add beef to tomato mixture. Simmer for 2 hours. Add beans and salt and cook until beans are heated through. Serves 8-10.

SOYBEANS IN TOMATO SAUCE

Soybeans are triglyceride fighters, so 'tri' them.

3 cups cooked soybeans
1 tablespoon butter or margarine
2 cups or 1 (15 to 16-ounce)
  can tomatoes
1 teaspoon cinnamon
2 teaspoons onion
1 tablespoon chopped parsley
  (optional)

1 tablespoon chopped
  green pepper
2 tablespoons honey
1 teaspoon salt, if canned
  chopped meat is
  not used
1 cup chopped canned meat or
  cooked ham

Mix all ingredients in a greased baking dish, stirring in meat last. Bake for 20 minutes in 350-degree oven.

SOYBEANS AND RICE

2 1/4 cups water
3/4 cup rice (do not wash)
1 tablespoon butter or
  margarine

3/4 teaspoon salt
1 cup cooked soybeans
1/2 cup grated cheese

Bring water to boiling. Add rice, butter, salt and soybeans. Bring to boiling again. Stir to keep rice from sticking until it boils. Reduce heat. Simmer 12 minutes. Reduce heat to very low so rice will steam done, about 8-10 minutes. Add cheese, and stir carefully to melt cheese. Serves 6.

The soybean is the only complete protein legume. Other legumes need cereal, grains, nuts, rice or dairy products to complete their nutrient value.

SOYBEAN CASSEROLE

2 cups cooked soybeans,
  chopped or whole
1/4 cup diced salt pork or fat
2 cups chopped celery
2 tablespoons chopped onion
2 tablespoons chopped green
  pepper

6 tablespoons flour
2 cups milk (or cooking water
  plus 2/3 cup dry milk)
1 teaspoon salt
1 cup buttered bread crumbs

Brown the salt pork in a frying pan. Add the celery, onion, and green pepper, and cook for about 5 minutes. Add thickening made from the flour, milk, and salt, and stir until it reaches the boiling point. Stir in the cooked beans and pour the mixture into a greased baking dish. Cover with buttered bread crumbs. Bake in a moderate oven (350 degrees) for about 30 minutes or until the crumbs are brown. Serves 6-8.

SOYBEANS AU GRATIN

2 1/2 cups cooked soybeans
1 tablespoon butter or margarine
2 teaspoons minced onion

1/2 cup grated cheese
1 cup White Sauce
2 tablespoons dry bread crumbs

To cooked soybeans add butter, onion, and cheese and white sauce. Melt cheese. Add soybeans. Pour into well-oiled casserole. Cover with bread crumbs. Bake in 350-degree oven until sauce bubbles and crumbs brown. Serves 4-5.

WHITE SAUCE:

2 tablespoons flour
1 cup water

1/3 cup dry milk

Mix together flour, water and milk in pan. Bring to boil and cook 5 minutes over low heat.

BEAN SPROUTS WITH RICE

1 cup garlic, minced
3 green onions, chopped
  with tops
2 teaspoon sesame seeds
1 cup prepared bean sprouts,
  drained

1 teaspoon oil
2 cups rice
3 tablespoons soy sauce
3 cups cold water

Mix garlic, onions, sesame seeds, and bean sprouts in saucepan. Pour oil over mixture and cook over medium heat, stirring constantly. Add soy sauce and water. Cover pot, bring to boil. Turn heat to low and allow to steam half an hour until rice is tender and liquid evaporates. Serve hot. Serves 6.

PEANUT CHOPS

An excellent meat substitute for a main dish.

6 slices rye bread, cut in half-triangles	1/2 teaspoon salt
	1/8 teaspoon paprika
1 cup smooth peanut butter	2 eggs
3/4 cup milk	Finely crushed cracker crumbs

Cut crust from bread and cut diagonally. Spread peanut butter on each side of bread. Add milk and seasonings to beaten eggs. Dip bread pieces in mixture, then in cracker crumbs. Bake in buttered casserole on 400 degrees for 10 minutes or until brown. Serves 6.

SOUTHERN STYLE GREEN BEANS

Daughter-in-law Deb perfers Kentucky Wonders for her favorite bean pot.

2 pounds fresh green beans	1 garlic clove
1/4 pound salt pork	1 teaspoon sugar
1/2 teaspoon salt	1 medium onion, chopped
1/4 teaspoon pepper	Water

Trim beans. Place all ingredients in 4-quart saucepan with water to barely cover. Bring to a boil and reduce to medium heat. Cook until tender. 'Real Southern' means long cooking—no al-dente here. Serves 6-8.

Variation: Add 1 (28-ounce) can tomatoes chopped, 1/4 cup chopped celery, and 1/4 cup chopped green peppers.

Variation: Cook peeled new potatoes on top of beans.

Peas and green beans like mushrooms, rosemary, dill, and thyme (not too much). Add 'crunch' with water chestnuts, pine nuts, almonds, or French fried onions.

STRING BEAN CASSEROLE

4 slices bacon, diced
2 medium onions, chopped
3 (#2) cans string beans
1 tablespoon caraway seeds
1 can cream of celery soup
1 cup grated Cheddar cheese

Salt and pepper to taste
1 cup cracker crumbs
  (saltines or Ritz)
1/2 stick butter or margarine
Paprika

Fry bacon. Drain. Reserve 2 tablespoons fat. Sauté onions until tender. Drain. Mix beans, onions, caraway seeds, bacon, soup, cheese, and seasonings. Cover with cracker crumbs. Dot with butter. Sprinkle with paprika. Bake 45 minutes at 350 degrees. Serves 8.

PICKLED GREEN BEANS

Add to salads, serve as party pickups, or simply use as pickles.

4 pounds whole green beans,
  stemmed and cut
1/4 teaspoon crushed red
  pepper (per jar)
1/2 teaspoon mustard seed
  (per jar)

1 clove garlic (per jar)
1/2 teaspoon dill seed
  (per jar)
5 cups vinegar
5 cups water
1/2 cup salt

Wash beans thoroughly. Drain. Pack in hot pint jars. Add pepper, mustard seed, garlic and dill to each jar. Combine vinegar, water, and salt. Bring mixture to boil and pour over beans, leaving 1/2 inch at top of jar. Seal. Process in boiling water 5 minutes. Cool. Store. Makes 7 pints.

Margarine can be substituted for butter in most recipes.

FAR EAST GREEN BEANS

4 cups fresh green beans, cut
1/2 pound lean beef, minced
3 tablespoons soy sauce
2 tablespoons sesame seeds

1 1/2 teaspoons sugar
2 green onions, chopped
2 teaspoons sesame oil

Wash and stem beans. Cut in 2-inch lengths. Parboil in water to
barely cover for 5 minutes. Set aside. Place chopped meat in skillet; add soy sauce, sesame seeds, sugar, onions, and oil. Stir fry until meat is tender. Drain beans and add to meat mixture. Cook just
until beans are tender, but do not overcook. Serves 6-8.

OLD PLANTERS SWEET AND SOUR
GREEN BEANS

*The Old Planters Restaurant is located in historic Hannibal,
Missouri.*

1 pound fresh green beans, cut
1 pod garlic
1 tablespoon oil
1 medium onion, chopped

1/2 cup brown sugar
1/2 cup vinegar
4 slices bacon, fried crisp and
  crumbled

Cook beans in salted water with 1 pod of garlic—15 minutes for
crisp-tender or longer to taste. Drain beans. Set aside. Heat oil.
Sauté onions until tender. Add sugar and vinegar. Heat for 1 minute. Pour over beans. Heat additional 3 minutes. Sprinkle with
crumbled bacon bits. Serves 4-6.

STIR-FRIED GARLIC GREEN BEANS

For lovers of crisp 'veggies.'

1 pound fresh green beans
6 cloves garlic
4 tablespoons oil

1/2 teaspoon salt
1 tablespoon light soy sauce
1 teaspoon sugar

Remove stems from beans, cut in half. Crush garlic coarsely. Heat
oil in wok or heavy skillet. Add beans and garlic, stir fry 5 minutes
on very high heat. (Edges of beans will singe slightly.) Add salt,
soy sauce, and sugar; stir to mix. Remove from heat and serve
immediately. Serves 4.

GREEN BEANS IN BACON SAUCE

1 pound fresh green beans
6 slices bacon
2 tablespoons flour
1 1/2 cups milk

2 tablespoons vinegar
1 tablespoon onion juice
1/2 cup cream

Stem, trim and cut green beans. Cook in salted water until tender. Fry bacon until crisp; drain, and reserve 2 tablespoons of fat. In heated fat, add flour, and stir until light brown. Stir in milk, vinegar and onion juice. Heat until thickened, about 3 minutes. Stir in cream. Place drained, cooked beans in serving dish and cover with sauce. Serves 6.

COMPANY-COMING GREEN BEAN CASSEROLE

1 cup sour cream
1/2 pound Swiss cheese,
   shredded
1/2 teaspoon salt
1/4 teaspoon pepper
2 teaspoons onion flakes
1 teaspoon brown sugar

1 tablespoon butter
2 teaspoons flour
1 teaspoon brown sugar
2 (16-ounce) cans whole green
   beans, drained
Seasoned bread crumbs

Fold sour cream into cheese. Mix well. Add seasonings. Make a roux of melted butter, flour, and brown sugar by heating together in small skillet. Fold into sour cream mixture. Butter a 2-quart baking dish. Place well-drained beans on bottom of casserole. Cover with sour cream mixture. Sprinkle with seasoned bread crumbs. Bake in 375-degree oven for 20 minutes. Serves 6-8.

GREEN BEANS PARMESAN

2 cups water
1 teaspoon salt
1 pound fresh green snap beans
2 tablespoons minced parsley
2 tablespoons butter

1/2 cup fresh grated Parmesan
   cheese
Freshly ground pepper
   to taste

In 2-quart saucepan, bring 2 cups water to a boil. Add salt and cut green beans. Cook 3 minutes uncovered to retain green color.

Then cover and cook on medium heat until beans are crisp-tender, about 20 minutes. Add parsley. Add butter, stirring to melt, then sprinkle with cheese and pepper. Stir, cook an additional 2-3 minutes until cheese melts slightly. Serves 4.

GREEN BEAN LOAF

1 can cooked green peas, mashed
1 cup cooked green beans, cut in
  small pieces
1 egg, slightly beaten
1 cup soft bread crumbs

2 tablespoons melted butter
  or margarine
1/2 teaspoon paprika
Salt and pepper to taste

Mix all ingredients. Place in greased baking dish. Bake 30 minutes in 375-degree oven. Loaf should be firm. Slice to serve. A white sauce is good to spoon on top. Serves 6.

KENTUCKY WONDER SHELL-OUTS

Toward the end of the season, Kentucky Wonder beans can produce enough beans in the pod to fill a pot. Most cooks like to mix a few 'snaps' with the shell-outs.

6 slices bacon
2 cups shell-outs
2 cups beans, snapped
3 quarts water

Salt and freshly ground pepper
  to taste
2 tablespoons chopped green
  onions

Fry bacon until crisp. Drain. Crumble and set aside. Reserve 2 tablespoons of bacon fat. Place beans, water, seasoning, and onions in 4-quart container. Simmer until beans are tender, 30-45 minutes. Drain. Blend bacon fat into beans; add crumbled bacon. Serves 6.

Your body digests beans slowly. After eating beans you will have a steady source of energy.

GREEN BEAN AND CORN CASSEROLE

1 (16-ounce) can French-style
  green beans
1 (12-ounce) can whole kernel
  corn
1/2 cup chopped onions
1/2 cup grated Cheddar cheese

1 can cream of mushroom soup
1/2 cup sour cream
1 roll Ritz crackers
1/2 cup slivered almonds
1/2 cup margarine

Drain beans and corn. Add onions, cheese, soup, and sour cream.
Pour into buttered casserole dish. Crumble crackers on top of casserole, then add almonds. Pour butter over top. Bake 35 minutes
in 350-degree oven. Serves 6.

STRING BEANS SAVOY

2 tablespoons vegetable oil
1 large onion, chopped
2 cups tomato juice
2 cloves garlic, crushed
1 teaspoon sugar

1 teaspoon salt
1/4 teaspoon pepper
Dash of cayenne pepper
2 (16-ounce) cans whole green
  beans, drained

Heat oil in medium-size skillet. Sauté onion until tender. Add tomato juice and seasonings Simmer 5 minutes. Pour over drained
beans. Cook 15 minutes. Serves 6.

SWEETS

PEANUT BUTTER CUPCAKES

1/4 cup butter
1/2 cup brown sugar
1/4 cup creamy peanut butter
1 egg, beaten until light
1 teaspoon vanilla

1 cup plain flour
1/4 teaspoon salt
1 teaspoon baking powder
1/2 cup milk

Beat softened butter and brown sugar until light and fluffy. Blend in peanut butter, egg and vanilla.

Sift flour, salt, and baking powder. Add sifted ingredients alternately three times with milk.

Bake in muffin tins 25 minutes in pre-heated 350-degree oven.

May be iced with Peanut Butter Icing made by mixing:

2 tablespoons butter
2 tablespoons peanut butter

2 tablespoons honey
1/2 cup confectioners' sugar

Spread on muffins while warm. Makes about 1 dozen muffins.

LENTIL APPLE CAKE

1/4 cup margarine	3/4 cup sugar
2 eggs	1 teaspoon cinnamon
2 cups mashed, cooked lentils	1/4 teaspoon nutmeg
1/2 cup whole wheat flour	1/4 teaspoon cloves
1/2 cup white enriched	2 cups diced peeled apples
all-purpose flour	1/2 cup chopped walnuts
1/4 teaspoon salt	1 1/2 teaspoons vanilla
1 teaspoon baking soda	

Cream margarine. Add eggs one at a time, beating well after each addition. Blend in lentils. In a small mixing bowl, combine flours (stir before measuring) with other dry ingredients and stir until well mixed. Add dry ingredient mixture to creamed mixture, blending well. Fold in apples, nuts and vanilla. Pour into greased and floured 9x13-inch pan. Bake at 350 degrees for 30-40 minutes. Ice with a cream cheese frosting. Makes 20 pieces.

EXTRA-CRISP PEANUT BUTTER COOKIES

1 cup butter	2 teaspoons soda
1 cup sugar	1/2 teaspoon salt
1 cup brown sugar	2 teaspoons vanilla
2 eggs	2/3 cup peanut butter, crunchy
2 2/3 cups plain flour	or plain

Cream butter; add sugars gradually and beat until fluffy. Add eggs, one at a time, beating mixture smooth. Combine flour, soda and salt. Add to cream mixture, beating to blend smooth. Stir in vanilla and peanut butter. Chill dough 1-2 hours. Pinch off enough dough for small, 1-inch ball. Place on cookie sheet. Bake in preheated 375-degree oven for 10-15 minutes. Cool before removing from cookie sheet. Makes about 6 dozen.

TOP OF THE STOVE PEANUT COOKIES

Surprising method for a quick and good snack.

2 tablespoons cocoa	1/4 cup peanut butter
2 cups sugar	1 teaspoon vanilla
1 stick butter or margarine	2 cups quick oats
1/2 cup milk	1 cup chopped peanuts

Mix cocoa, sugar, butter, and milk in medium-size saucepan. Boil hard 1 1/2 minutes. Remove from heat. Add remaining ingredients. Mix well. Drop by spoonfuls on waxed paper. Makes 2 dozen cookies.

CHICKPEA CRISPY COOKIES

Don't be a doubting Thomas—you will be pleasantly surprised when you sample these goodies.

1 1/4 cups plain flour	1 can drained garbanzo
2 teaspoons baking powder	(chickpea) beans
1/2 teaspoon allspice	1 cup milk
1/2 teaspoon ginger	1 stick butter
1/2 teaspoon salt	3/4 cup brown sugar (packed)
1/4 cup orange juice concentrate	1 egg
1/2 teaspoon vanilla	Powdered sugar for dusting

Sift together flour, baking powder, spices, and salt. Place orange juice, vanilla, beans, and milk in blender. Purée until smooth.

In large bowl, cream butter and brown sugar until fluffy. Beat in egg. Blend in purée mixture. Add dry ingredients until smooth. Spoon by teaspoonfuls on lightly greased cookie sheets. Bake in preheated 375-degree oven until browned around edges. Makes about 3 dozen cookies.

For cookie recipes, always pack brown sugar firmly unless recipe specifies otherwise.

PRESIDENT'S FAVORITE PEANUT BRITTLE

(Jimmy Carter's, that is—using his own homegrown Georgia peanuts, no doubt.)

3 cups sugar
1 1/2 cups water
1 cup white corn syrup
3 cups raw peanuts

2 tablespoons soda
1/2 stick butter
1 teaspoon vanilla

Boil sugar, water, and syrup until it will spin a thread from a spoon. Add peanuts. Stir until syrup becomes golden brown. Remove from heat; add soda, butter and vanilla. Stir until butter melts. Pour on 2 cookie sheets (with sides). As mixture hardens around edge, pull to thin. Break when cool to touch.

PEANUT BUTTER CANDY

1/2 cup crunchy peanut butter
1/3 cup honey

3/4 cup wheat germ
1 tablespoon instant nonfat milk

Mix all ingredients. Drop by teaspoonfuls on waxed paper. Chill in refrigerator. Makes 10-12 pieces.

SWEET BEAN PIE

1 (16-ounce) can navy beans,
  drained
1/4 cup melted margarine
  or butter
3 eggs, beaten
3/4 cup sugar

2 teaspoons vanilla
1/8 teaspoon salt
1 (9-inch) unbaked pie shell
Whipped cream
Cinnamon or nutmeg

Mash beans, add margarine, eggs, sugar, vanilla and salt. Beat until smooth. Pour in pie shell. Bake at 350 degrees for 45 minutes. Serve with whipped cream sprinkled with cinnamon or nutmeg.
Variation: Substitute 1 cup cooked pinto beans for navy beans. Add 1 teaspoon cinnamon.

LIMA BEAN PIE

Reserve comments until after you have tried this delightful taste.

1/2 cup sugar
1 tablespoon flour
1/2 teaspoon salt
1 teaspoon ground ginger
1 teaspoon ground cinnamon
1 teaspoon ground nutmeg
1/8 teaspoon ground cloves
1/4 cup soft margarine

1 1/2 cups mashed, cooked
  green lima beans
1/2 cup white corn syrup
3 eggs
1 cup evaporated milk
1 (9-inch) unbaked pie shell,
  chilled
Whipped cream topping

Mix sugar, flour and spices. Blend margarine, lima beans, and syrup; add lima mixture to flour mix. Stir until smooth. Beat in eggs, one at a time. Stir in milk. Pour mixture into unbaked shell. Bake in preheated 350-degree oven 1-hour, until knife inserted in center comes out clean. Serve with whipped cream topping. Serves 6-8.

PEANUT BUTTER CREAM PIE

1 (6-ounce) package cream cheese
1 cup powdered sugar
1/2 cup crunchy peanut butter

1 (9-ounce) carton commercial
  topping or whipped cream
1 graham cracker crust

Cream the cream cheese with sugar and peanut butter until well blended, adding a little milk if mixture is too thick. Fold in 1/2 of cream and pour into pie shell. Refrigerate until set. Keep refrigerated until served. Cover with remaining whipped cream. Serves 6-7.

Salt added when soaking tends to toughen dried beans during the cooking period.

SOUTHERN PEANUT PIE

3 eggs, beaten
1 cup dark syrup
1/2 cup sugar
2 tablespoons butter, melted

1 teaspoon vanilla
1 cup salted peanuts
1 unbaked (9-inch) pie shell
Whipped cream or ice cream

Beat eggs, syrup, sugar, butter and vanilla. Stir in peanuts and pour into shell. Bake at 350 degrees for 45 minutes. Serve with whipped cream or vanilla ice cream. Serves 6-8.

PEANUT BUTTER CUSTARD PIE

What goes around comes around.

(This recipe won me a state award in the first national cooking contest I entered.)

2 cups milk
1/3 cup sugar
1/3 cup flour
1/4 teaspoon salt
2 egg yolks, beaten
1/2 teaspoon vanilla

1/2 cup creamy peanut butter
1 prepared pie shell or cookie
  crumb shell
Whipped cream and chopped
  peanuts for garnish

Scald 1 1/2 cups milk; add small amount to mixture of sugar, flour, and salt. Add this mixture to scalded milk. Cook 15 minutes, stirring constantly. Mix small amount of mixture to eggs. Add mixture to thickening milk mixture. Cook until thickened. Set aside to cool. Mix remaining milk with peanut butter; fold into custard mix. Pour in pie shell. Top with whipped cream. Sprinkle crushed peanuts on top. Serves 6-8.

MISCELLANEOUS

BROWN BEAN BREAD

1 (15-ounce) can kidney beans
1/3 cup vegetable oil
1/3 cup smooth peanut butter
1/3 cup molasses
3 tablespoons brown sugar
1 teaspoon salt
1 egg

3 packages active yeast
1 cup hot water
1 cup whole wheat flour
4 cups plain flour
1/2 to 2 cups flour
Egg white

Blend beans, oil, peanut butter, molasses, sugar, salt, and egg in mixer on low speed for 3 minutes. Place in large mixing bowl. Mix yeast and hot water to dissolve. Add to bean mixture. Begin working in whole wheat and 4 cups plain flour. Add enough of remaining plain flour to make a stiff dough. Knead mixture with hands until dough is smooth and elastic with a shine to the surface. Let stand, covered, until dough doubles, 1-2 hours.

Punch down and let sit 15 minutes. Knead and shape into 2 round loaves. Place on greased cookie sheet. Brush with beaten egg white. Slash across tops of loaves. Bake in preheated 350-degree oven for 1 hour until bread sounds hollow when tapped.

91

PURPLE HULL PEA JELLY

This jelly has a lovely pale lavender color and the taste of muscadine jelly.

Pea hulls from 2 pounds purple   2 quarts water
  hull peas (washed and rinsed)

Place hulls in water, cover and boil for 10 minutes. Reduce heat and simmer 45-50 minutes. Strain through fine strainer.

4 cups pea juice   5 cups sugar
1 box powdered pectin   Juice of 1 lemon

Mix juice and pectin. Bring to a rolling boil. Add sugar and lemon juice; stir to dissolve. Bring to a rolling boil that cannot be stirred down. Boil 15 minutes. Remove from heat, skim off foam. Pour into sterilized jars, seal, and process 5 minutes in a boiling water bath canner. Makes 4-6 pints.

SAVORY SPLIT PEA PANCAKES

An unusual nutty flavor—a healthy breakfast treat.

1 cup green or yellow split peas,   1 egg, well-beaten
  rinsed and drained   1/4 cup all-purpose flour
2 cups water   1 teaspoon salt
1 cup finely chopped onion   1/2 teaspoon pepper
2 garlic cloves,   Yogurt or sour cream for gar-
  minced   nish

In saucepan, combine split peas and water. Cover; bring to boil. Reduce heat; simmer 30-35 minutes or until peas are tender. Cool slightly. Stir in onion, garlic, egg, flour, salt and pepper. Heat a skillet or griddle over high heat; coat lightly with oil or cooking spray. Drop batter by large spoonfuls onto hot skillet; spread batter evenly. Cook until surface bubbles burst; edges will look slightly dry. Turn pancakes and cook until underside is golden. Garnish with yogurt or sour cream. Serves 4 (12 pancakes).

BAKED BEAN SANDWICHES

3 hot dog buns, halved
Butter or margarine
1 (16-ounce) can baked beans
  or 2 cups leftover beans

3-4 tablespoons catsup
1/4 cup shredded cheese
6 slices bacon

Toast buns. Spread both tops and bottoms with butter. Top with beans, catsup and cheese. Lay bacon pieces on top. Broil 3 inches from heat, until bacon is crisp.

PEANUT BUTTER TOAST

1 1/2 cups smooth peanut butter
1 1/2 cups hot milk
1 teaspoon salt

3 tablespoons butter or
  margarine
6 slices bread

Thoroughly mix peanut butter, milk, and salt. Heat butter in skillet. Dip slices of bread in peanut mixture. Sauté in hot butter, turning once. Serve with syrup as a breakfast dish or a side dish for a vegetarian meal.

BOILED PEANUTS

Choose fresh, green peanuts. Wash until clean and place in large pot with enough water to cover 2 inches above the peanuts. Add 1/3 cup salt to begin with, then by tasting. Boil peanuts 3-4 hours until soft to taste. If allowed to sit, peanuts will get saltier. Otherwise, drain and cool.

HOMEMADE PEANUT BUTTER

1 pound shelled, unroasted	1 tablespoon salt (optional)
peanuts, skins removed	1 tablespoon Tahini (optional)
1/4 cup wheat germ	(Sesame seed paste)

Preheat oven to 300 degrees. Place peanuts in greased baking sheet. Bake 10-15 minutes, stirring occasionally, until golden brown. Place peanuts and all ingredients in blender. Blend until smooth. Yields enough for 6 sandwiches.

BEAN CURD

If you have the urge to do something from scratch—make your own tofu!

| 2 1/2 cups soybeans | 2 tablespoons vinegar |
| 6 cups water | |

Cover beans with 3 cups of water and allow to soak at least 6 hours. Drain and rinse well. Place 1/3 of beans in a food processor with 1/2 cup of water. Process until smooth. Continue adding beans in thirds with water until all are processed smooth. Add remaining water.

Place beans in a cheesecloth in a colander over a large utensil. Tie ends of cloth and squeeze liquid from beans. Leave for several hours and continue to squeeze milk from beans. Place liquid over high heat, bring to boil for 5 minutes. Cool and skim top. Add vinegar. Curds will begin to form. Cover and let set until cool.

Place curds in clean cheesecloth and drain as before. Place on flat dish, cover with flat dish, and weigh down with a can or two. Leave for 4 hours; drain, add fresh water. Will keep for a week by changing water daily. Makes about 1 1/2 cups of curd.

BEAN SPROUTS

Salads, sandwiches, and stir-fry foods will take on a new taste dimension with the addition of bean sprouts. It is not hard to grow your own. Just be sure you sprout from beans that are for human consumption. Mung beans and soybeans, readily available in specialty food stores, are excellent to sprout beans, but it is entirely possible with black-eyed peas, chickpeas, lentils, and even dried corn kernels.

Wash and rinse well 1/2 cup dried beans of choice. Place in clean quart jar, add warm water to almost the top of the jar; and let soak overnight. Cover with a strainer or porous material and secure with a rubber band. Drain well, place in a dark place (pantry or cabinet). Rinse at least twice a day. With chickpeas it will take several more rinsings. Continue the storage and rinsing until sprouts are the desired length. You can buy canned bean sprouts, and fresh ones in the produce department, but there is a great deal of satisfaction in growing your own.

SOY MAYONNAISE

Excellent (no cholesterol) for green salads.

1/2 cup soy flour	1/8 teaspoon cayenne pepper
1 cup water	1 teaspoon grated onion
1/2 teaspoon salt	1 cup oil
1/2 teaspoon paprika	1/4 cup lemon juice

Place soy flour, water, salt, paprika, cayenne, and onions in blender. Blend until smooth. Turn blender to high, adding oil drop by drop until mixture begins to thicken. Add lemon juice. Chill. Makes 2 cups.

TOFU DRESSING

Tofu is available in most large supermarkets today. Serve this dressing over green salads, bean sprouts, or cooked vegetables.

1 (4-inch) square bean curd (tofu)	1/2 cup salad oil
1/2 teaspoon minced fresh ginger	1/2 cup cider vinegar
or 1 teaspoon ground ginger	Tabasco sauce to taste
Salt to taste	

Place all ingredients in blender. Adjust seasonings. Use immediately or store in refrigerator. Bring to room temperature before using to mix oil. Makes about 1 cup.

TABLES

EQUIVALENTS: FOOD

Food	Quantity	Yield
Dry beans	1 cup	2 1/2 cups cooked
Bread crumbs	1 slice bread	3/4 cup soft crumbs
Bread crumbs	3-4 slices	1 cup dry crumbs
Cheese	1/4 pound	1 cup shredded
Crackers	16	1 cup coarse crumbs
Peanuts	5 ounces	1 cup
Onions	1 medium	1/2 cup chopped
Rice	1 cup	3 1/2 cups cooked

EQUIVALENTS: BEANS, PEAS

1 pound beans or peas in shell	=	1/2 pound shelled, (4 cups)
1 cup beans	=	1 1/2 cups creamed
1 pound limas	=	2 cups
1 1/2 pounds peanut meats	=	3 cups chopped
1 cup chopped peanuts	=	5 ounces
1 cup ground peanuts	=	1 cup or 8 ounces

EQUIVALENTS: PEANUTS

1 pound peanuts in shell	=	2/3 pound or 2 1/3 cups shelled
1 pound shelled peanuts	=	3 1/4 cups
1 1/2 pounds unshelled, roasted peanuts	=	1 pound shelled nuts
1 pound peanut butter	=	2 cups
1 pound peanut oil	=	2 cups

CALORIES: BEANS, PEAS

Baked beans, canned with sugar or molasses	1 cup	=	325
Baked beans, canned with tomato sauce	1 cup	=	295
Fresh green beans with seasoning	1 cup	=	35
Canned green beans	1 cup	=	45
Kidney beans	1 cup	=	230
Fresh lima beans, seasoned	1 cup	=	160
Lima beans, canned	1 cup	=	152
Lima beans, dry, cooked	1 cup	=	260
Lima beans, frozen, cooked	1 cup	=	270
Navy beans , dry	1 cup	=	321
Pinto beans, dry	1 cup	=	349
Wax beans, canned	1 cup	=	27
Fresh green peas, cooked	1 cup	=	110
Green peas, canned	1 cup	=	170
Green peas, frozen	1 cup	=	150

CALORIES: PEANUTS

Peanut butter	1 tablespoon	= 90
Peanuts, Spanish	1/4 cup	= 40

WEIGHTS AND MEASURES

A pinch or dash	=	1/8 teaspoon or less
1 tablespoon	=	3 teaspoons
4 tablespoons	=	1/4 cup
8 tablespoons	=	1/2 cup
12 tablespoons	=	3/4 cup
1 cup of liquid	=	1/2 pint
2 cups of liquid	=	1 pint
4 cups of liquid	=	1 quart
2 pints of liquid	=	1 quart
4 quarts	=	1 gallon
16 ounces	=	1 pound
1 quart green beans	=	3 1/4 pounds
1 cup dried beans	=	1/2 pound

AVERAGE CAN EQUIVALENTS

No. 1	=	1 1/3 cups or 10 ounces
No. 300	=	1 3/4 cups or 16 ounces
No. 303	=	2 cups or 16-17 ounces
No. 2	=	2 1/2 cups or 20 ounces
No. 2 1/2	=	3 1/2 cups or 28 ounces
No. 3	=	4 cups or 32 ounces
No. 10	=	13 cups or 116 ounces

INDEX

A

Appetizer:
  Bean Spread for Cocktail
    Crackers 20
  Black Bean Dip 16
  Black-Eyed Pea Nachos 19
  Chickpea Spread 18
  Greek Bean Dip 16
  Green Bean Canapés 20
  Hummus 16
  Lucky Black-Eyed Pea Dip 15
  Mexicali Bean Dip 17
  Mississippi Caviar 17
  Nigerian Bean Balls 19
  Peanut Balls 19
  Refried-Bean Dip 17
  Spicy Bean Dip 15
  Stuffed Snow Peas 18
Authentic Red Beans and Rice 55
Author's Favorite Red Beans and
  Rice 55

B

Baked Bean Sandwiches 93
Baked Beans 5 A.M. 51
Baked Beans for a Crowd 49
Baked Beans with Plum
  Preserves 49
Baked Peanut Loaf 75
Barbecued Baked Beans 48
Barbecued Limas 68
Bayou Bean Salad 40
Bean Chalupas 66
Bean Curd 94
Bean Pot 51
Bean Salad in Pocket Bread 38

Bean Salad with Tuna 38
Bean Spread for Cocktail
  Crackers 20
Bean Sprouts 94
Bean Sprouts with Rice 78
Bean Taco Salad 39
Black Beans:
  and Rice, California 70
  Dip 16
  in Wine 70
  Paprika Soup 26
  Sauce for Beef or Pork 33
  Sauce for Fish 32
  Soup, Creole 26
  Soup, Delta Queen 25
Black-Eyed Peas:
  and Tomatoes 62
  Dip 16
  Hoppin' John 63
  Mississippi Caviar 17
  Nachos 19
  Nigerian Bean Balls 19
  Ole Fashion 61
  Patties 61
  Salad 40
  Soup 22
  Spiced 61
  Three-Bean Soup with Crab
    Boil 23
  with Salsa 62
Boiled Peanuts 93
Boston Baked Beans with Maple
  Syrup 48
Brandied Navy Beans 72
Broccoli-Lentil Salad 43
Brown Bean Bread 91

C

Cake, Lentil Apple 86
California Black Beans and
Rice 70
Capitol Hill Bean Soup 30
Carameled Lima Beans 70
Chickpea Spread 18
Chickpeas:
Casserole 59
Chili Con Lentils 57
Cookies, Crispy 87
Hummus 16
Quick and Spicy 56
Spread 18
Chili Con Lentils 57
Chili Pie with Beans 64
Chinese Pea Pods 74
Classic Red Beans and Rice 53
Company-Coming Green Bean
Casserole 82
Cowboy Beer Beans 60
Cowboy Pot Roast with Beans 67
Creole Black Bean Soup 26
Crispy Chickpea Cookies 87
Crockpot Red Beans 63
Crunchy Green Pea Salad 42
Cupcakes, Peanut Butter 85
Curried Lentils From India 58

D

Delta Baked Beans 48
Delta Queen Black Bean Soup 25

E

Easy Sweet Pea Salad 42
Extra-Crisp Peanut Butter
Cookies 85

F

Fiesta Pea Salad 43
Fresh Green Pea Pie 73
Fresh Green Pea Soup 23

G

Garbanzo (See Chickpeas)
Garbanzo Sauce for Spaghetti 33
Great Northern Beans:
Bean Salad with Tuna 38
Picnic Baked Beans 50
White Beans Provençal 72
Greek Bean Dip 16
Greek Garbanzo Beans with
Anchovy 39
Green Beans:
and Corn Casserole 84
Bayou Bean Salad 40
Bean Pot 51
Canapés 20
Casserole, Company-Coming 82
Far East 81
in Bacon Sauce 82
Loaf 83
Marinated Bean Salad 38
Old Planters Sweet and Sour 81
Parmesan 82
Pickled 80
Salad 37
Southern Style 79
Stir-Fried Garlic 81
String Bean Casserole 80
String Bean Savoy 84
String Bean Soup 26
Green Pea Pasta Salad Primavera 41
Green Peas:
Orange-Pea Salad 42
Pasta Salad Primavera 41
Pea Pod Soup 28
Pie, Fresh 73
Salad, Crunchy 42
Soup, Fresh 23

H

Haddow Soup 24
Herbed Lentil and Rice Salad 45
Homemade Peanut Butter 94

Hoppin' John 63
Hummus 15

I

Italian Bean Sauce for Pasta 34
Italian Bean Soup with Pasta 21
Italian Cannellini Beans 71

K

Kentucky Wonder Shell-Outs 83
Kidney Beans:
  Barbecued Baked Beans 48
  Bean Pot 51
  Bean Taco Salad 39
  Beef, Beans, and Macaroni
    Chili 76
  Brown Bean Bread 91
  Chili Con Lentils 57
  Chili Pie with Beans 64
  Cowboy Pot Roast with Beans 67
  Crockpot Red Beans 63
  Louisiana Red Beans 54
  Red Bean Supper Dish 59
  Red Beans Bourguignon 65
  Salad 40
  Spicy Bean Dip 15
  Tailgate Chili 76
  Tex-Mex Chili with Beans 29
  Three-Bean Soup with Crab
    Boil 23

L

Lentils:
  Vegetable Stir-Fry, Red 57
  Apple Cake 86
  Broccoli-Lentil Salad 43
  Chili Con 57
  Confetti Salad 44
  Curried Lentil Rice Salad 44
  From India, Curried 58
  Patties 58
  Pilaf 59

Soup with Frankfurters 27
Spaghetti Sauce 32
Stew 27
Lima Beans:
  Barbecued Baked Beans 48
  Barbecued Limas 68
  Carameled 70
  Curry 69
  Mock Sausage 67
  Pie 88
  Roast 68
  Salad 45
  Spanish Baked 69
  Tomato salad 46
  Traditional Bean Cassoulet 60
Louisiana Red Beans 54
Lucky Black-Eyed Pea Dip 15

M

Marinated Bean Salad 38
Meaty Red Beans and Rice 56
Mexicali Bean Dip 17
Mississippi Caviar 17
Missouri Sweet Pepper Relish for
  White Beans 35
Mixed Bean Relish 34
Mock Sausage 67

N

Navy Beans:
  Bean Spread for Cocktail
    Crackers 20
  Boston Baked Beans with Maple
    Syrup 48
  Brandied 72
  Capitol Hill Bean Soup 30
  Greek Bean Dip 16
  Italian Bean Sauce for Pasta 34
  New England Baked Beans 47
  Sweet Bean Pie 87
  Three-Bean Soup with Crab Boil
    23

New England Baked Beans 47
New Orleans Red Bean Soup 25
Nigerian Bean Balls 19

O

Old Planters Sweet and Sour Green
  Beans 81
Old-Fashioned Baked Beans 47
Ole Fashion Black-Eyed Peas 61
Orange-Pea Salad 42

P

Pea Pod Soup 28
Peanut Balls 19
Peanuts:
  Balls 19
  Barbecue Sauce for Venison 32
  Boiled 93
  Brittle, President's Favorite 88
  Butter Candy 88
  Butter Cream Pie 88
  Butter Cupcakes 85
  Butter Custard Pie 90
  Butter Toast 93
  Butter, Homemade 94
  Chops 79
  Extra-Crisp Peanut Butter
    Cookies 86
  Loaf, Baked 75
  Sauce 31
  Sauce, Gingered 31
  Scrapple 76
  Soup, Rich 28
  Pie, Southern 90
  Soup, Southern Diner 29
  Top of the Stove Peanut
    Cookies 86
Picnic Baked Beans 50
Pinto Bean Gumbo 31
Pinto Beans:
  Bean Chalupas 66
  Bean Salad in Pocket Bread 38
  Cowboy Beer Beans 60
  Real Chili 30

Savory 66
Pork and Beans:
  Baked Beans 5 A.M. 51
  Bean Pot 51
  Delta Baked Beans 48
  Old-Fashioned Baked Beans 47
  Spicy Baked Beans 50
  Spiked Baked Beans 50
President's Favorite Peanut
  Brittle 88
Purple Hull Pea Jelly 92

Q

Quick and Spicy Chickpeas 56

R

Real Chili 30
Red Beans:
  and Rice, Authentic 55
  and Rice, Author's Favorite 55
  and Rice, Classic 53
  and Rice, Meaty 56
  and Rice, Spicy 54
  Bourguignon 65
  Louisiana 54
  Mexicali Bean Dip 17
  Soup, New Orleans 25
  Supper Dish 56
Red Lentil-Vegetable Stir-Fry 57
Refried Beans 64
Refried Beans in Cornmeal Crepes 65
Refried-Bean Party Dip 17
Rich Peanut Soup 29

S

Salad:
  Bayou Bean 40
  Bean Salad in Pocket Bread 38
  Bean Salad with Tuna 38
  Bean Taco 39
  Black-Eyed Pea 40
  Broccoli-Lentil 43
  Crunchy Green Pea 42
  Curried Lentil Rice 44

102

Easy Sweet Pea 42
Fiesta Pea 43
Greek Garbanzo Beans with
  Anchovy 39
Green Bean 37
Green Pea Pasta Salad
  Primavera 41
Herbed Lentil and Rice 45
Kidney Bean 40
Lentil Confetti 44
Lima Bean 45
Lima Bean-Tomato 46
Marinated Bean 38
Orange-Pea 42
White Bean 41
Savory Pinto Beans 66
Savory Split Pea Pancakes 92
Soup:
  Black Bean Paprika 26
  Black-Eyed Pea 22
  Capitol Hill Bean 30
  Creole Black Bean 26
  Delta Queen Black Bean 25
  Fresh Green Pea 23
  Haddow 24
  Italian Bean Soup with Pasta 21
  Lentil Soup with Frankfurters 27
  Lentil Stew 27
  New Orleans Red Bean 25
  Pea Pod 28
  Rich Peanut 28
  Southern Diner Peanut 29
  Split Pea Soup Milano 24
  String Bean 26
  Three-Bean Soup with Crab
    Boil 23
  Vegetable Soy 22
Southern Diner Peanut Soup 29
Southern Peanut Pie 90
Southern Style Green Beans 79
Soy Mayonnaise 95
Soybeans:
  and Rice 77
  Au Gratin 78
  Bean Curd 94

Bean Sprouts 94
  Casserole 78
  in Tomato Sauce 77
  Vegetable Soybean Soup 22
Spanish Baked Lima Beans 69
Spiced Black-Eyed Peas 61
Spicy Baked Beans 50
Spicy Bean Dip 15
Spicy Red Beans and Rice 54
Spiked Baked Beans 50
Split Peas:
  Fiesta Pea Salad 43
  Green Pea Pasta Salad
    Primavera 41
  Italian Bean Soup with Pasta 21
  Pancakes, Savory 92
  Patties 74
  Soup 23
  Soup Milano 24
Stir-Fried Garlic Green Beans 81
Stir-Fried Pea Pods with Shrimp 73
String Bean Casserole 80
String Bean Soup 26
Stuffed Snow Peas 18
Sweet Bean Pie 88

T

Tailgate Chili 76
Taiwan Peas 74
Tex-Mex Chili with Beans 29
Three-Bean Soup with Crab Boil 23
Tofu Dressing 95
Top of the Stove Peanut Cookies 87
Traditional Bean Cassoulet 60

V

Vegetable Soybean Soup 22

W

White Bean Salad 41
White Beans Florence 71
White Beans Provençal 72
Wine Dressing for Bean Salads 37

ABOUT THE AUTHOR

A native of Tupelo, Mississippi, Margie F. Tyler received her BA degree from the University of Mississippi. She taught school in McComb and Pike County and found time to cook plenty of hearty food for her husband Bill and their three sons.

Margie turned to a serious pursuit of contest cooking following the death of her husband in 1975. She joined the winners circle in such prestigious cooking competitions as Pillsbury, Chicken, Beef, Pineapple, and Catfish, among others.

In 1976, when she 'temporarily' moved to Jackson., Mississippi, Margie joined the Mississippi Department of Economic Development as Special Events and Convention Coordinator. In 1979 she served as Project Coordinator for the First International Ballet Competition. After leaving the department in 1980, Margie established the full time office of the Mississippi Broadcasters Association. In 1984 she established Resources Unlimited, a consulting service for meetings, special events, and conventions.

When Margie isn't in the kitchen testing and creating recipes, she finds time to paint in water colors or add a chapter to her first romance novel. And she always is ready to open the mythical Tumble Inn for her three grandcihldren who think her Sour Cream Biscuits are the best.